Hyperion by Henry Wadsworth Longfellow

Henry Wadsworth Longfellow was born on February 27th, 1807 in Portland, Maine. As a young boy, it was obvious that he was very studious and he quickly became fluent in Latin.

He published his first poem, "The Battle of Lovell's Pond", in the Portland Gazette on November 17th, 1820. He was already thinking of a career in literature and, in his senior year, wrote to his father: "I will not disguise it in the least... the fact is, I most eagerly aspire after future eminence in literature, my whole soul burns most ardently after it, and every earthly thought centers in it...."

After graduation travels in Europe occupied the next three years and he seemed to easily absorb any language he set himself to learn.

On September 14th, 1831, Longfellow married Mary Storer Potter. They settled in Brunswick.

His first published book was in 1833, a translation of poems by the Spanish poet Jorge Manrique. He also published a travel book, Outre-Mer: A Pilgrimage Beyond the Sea.

During a trip to Europe Mary became pregnant. Sadly, in October 1835, she miscarried at some six months. After weeks of illness she died, at the age of 22 on November 29th, 1835. Longfellow wrote "One thought occupies me night and day... She is dead — She is dead! All day I am weary and sad".

In late 1839, Longfellow published Hyperion, a book in prose inspired by his trips abroad.

Ballads and Other Poems was published in 1841 and included "The Village Blacksmith" and "The Wreck of the Hesperus". His reputation as a poet, and a commercial one at that, was set.

On May 10th, 1843, after seven years in pursuit of a chance for new love, Longfellow received word from Fanny Appleton that she agreed to marry him.

On November 1st, 1847, the epic poem Evangeline was published.

In 1854, Longfellow retired from Harvard, to devote himself entirely to writing.

The Song of Haiwatha, perhaps his best known and enjoyed work was published in 1855.

On July 10th, 1861, after suffering horrific burns the previous day. In his attempts to save her Longfellow had also been badly burned and was unable to attend her funeral.

He spent several years translating Dante Alighieri's Divine Comedy. It was published in 1867.

Longfellow was also part of a group who became known as The Fireside Poets which also included William Cullen Bryant, John Greenleaf Whittier, James Russell Lowell, and Oliver Wendell Holmes Snr.

Longfellow was the most popular poet of his day. As a friend once wrote to him, "no other poet was so fully recognized in his lifetime". Some of his works including "Paul Revere's Ride" and "The Song of Haiwatha" may have rewritten the facts but became essential parts of the American psyche and culture.

Henry Wadsworth Longfellow died, surrounded by family, on Friday, March 24th, 1882. He had been suffering from peritonitis.

Index of Contents

BOOK I

Epigraph

"Who ne'er his bread in sorrow ate,
Who ne'er the mournful, midnight hours
Weeping upon his bed has sate,
He knows you not, ye Heavenly Powers."

CHAPTER I

THE HERO

In John Lyly's Endymion, Sir Topas is made to say; "Dost thou know what a Poet is? Why, fool, a Poet is as much as one should say,—a Poet!" And thou, reader, dost thou know what a hero is? Why, a hero is as much as one should say,—a hero! Some romance-writers, however, say much more than this. Nay, the old Lombard, Matteo Maria Bojardo, set all the church-bells in Scandiano ringing, merely because he had found a name for one of his heroes. Here, also, shall church-bells be rung, but more solemnly.

The setting of a great hope is like the setting of the sun. The brightness of our life is gone. Shadows of evening fall around us, and the world seems but a dim reflection,—itself a broader shadow. We look forward into the coming, lonely night. The soul withdraws into itself. Then stars arise, and the night is holy.

Paul Flemming had experienced this, though still young. The friend of his youth was dead. The bough had broken "under the burden of the unripe fruit." And when, after a season, he looked up again from the blindness of his sorrow, all things seemed unreal. Like the man, whose sight had been restored by miracle, he beheld men, as trees, walking. His household gods were broken. He had no home. His sympathies cried aloud from his desolate soul, and there came no answer from the busy, turbulent world around him. He did not willingly give way to grief. He struggled to be cheerful,—to be strong. But he could no longer look into the familiar faces of his friends. He could no longer live alone, where he had lived with her. He went abroad, that the sea might be between him and the grave. Alas! Between him and his sorrow there could be no sea, but that of time.

He had already passed many months in lonely wandering, and was now pursuing his way along the Rhine, to the south of Germany. He had journeyed the same way before, in brighter days and a brighter season of the year, in the May of life and in the month of May. He knew the beauteous river all by heart;—every rock and ruin, every echo, every legend. The ancient castles, grim and hoar, that had taken root as it were on the cliffs,—they were all his; for his thoughts dwelt in them, and the wind told him tales.

He had passed a sleepless night at Rolandseck, and had risen before daybreak. He opened the window of the balcony to hear the rushing of the Rhine. It was a damp December morning; and clouds were passing over the sky,—thin, vapory clouds, whose snow-white skirts were "often spotted with golden tears, which men call stars." The day dawned slowly; and, in the mingling of daylight and starlight, the island and cloister of Nonnenwerth made together but one broad, dark shadow on the silver breast of the river. Beyond, rose the summits of the Siebengebirg. Solemn and dark, like a monk, stood the Drachenfels, in his hood of mist, and rearward extended the Curtain of Mountains, back to the Wolkenburg,—the Castle of the Clouds.

But Flemming thought not of the scene before him. Sorrow unspeakable was upon his spirit in that lonely hour; and, hiding his face in his hands, he exclaimed aloud;

"Spirit of the past! look not so mournfully at me with thy great, tearful eyes! Touch me not with thy cold hand! Breathe not upon me with the icy breath of the grave! Chant no more that dirge of sorrow, through the long and silent watches of the night!"

Mournful voices from afar seemed to answer, "Treuenfels!" and he remembered how others had suffered, and his heart grew still.

Slowly the landscape brightened. Down the rushing stream came a boat, with its white wings spread, and darted like a swallow through the narrow pass of God's-Help. The boatmen were singing, but not the song of Roland the Brave, which was heard of old by the weeping Hildegund, as she sat within the walls of that cloister, which now looked forth in the pale morning from amid the leafless linden trees. The dim traditions of those gray old times rose in the traveller's memory; for the ruined tower of Rolandseck was still looking down upon the Kloster Nonnenwerth, as if the sound of the funeral bell had changed the faithful Paladin to stone, and he were watching still to see the form of his beloved one come forth, not from her cloister, but from her grave. Thus the brazen clasps of the book of legends were opened, and, on the page illuminated by the misty rays of the rising sun, he read again the tales of Liba, and the mournful bride of Argenfels, and Siegfried, the mighty slayer of the dragon. Meanwhile the mists had risen from the Rhine, and the whole air was filled with golden vapor, through which he beheld the sun, hanging in heaven like a drop of blood. Even thus shone the sun within him, amid the wintry vapors, uprising from the valley of the shadow of death, through which flowed the stream of his life,—sighing, sighing!

CHAPTER II

THE CHRIST OF ANDERNACH

Paul Flemming resumed his solitary journey. The morning was still misty, but not cold. Across the Rhine the sun came wading through the reddish vapors; and soft and silver-white outspread the broad river, without a ripple upon its surface, or visible motion of the ever-moving current. A little vessel, with one loose sail, was riding at anchor, keel to keel with another, that lay right under it, its own apparition,— and all was silent, and calm, and beautiful.

The road was for the most part solitary; for there are few travellers upon the Rhine in winter. Peasant women were at work in the vineyards; climbing up the slippery hill-sides, like beasts of burden, with large baskets of manure upon their backs. And once during the morning, a band of apprentices, with knapsacks, passed by, singing, "The Rhine! The Rhine! a blessing on the Rhine!"

O, the pride of the German heart in this noble river! And right it is; for, of all the rivers of this beautiful earth, there is none so beautiful as this. There is hardly a league of its whole course, from its cradle in the snowy Alps to its grave in the sands of Holland, which boasts not its peculiar charms. By heavens! If I were a German I would be proud of it too; and of the clustering grapes, that hang about its temples, as it reels onward through vineyards, in a triumphal march, like Bacchus, crowned and drunken.

But I will not attempt to describe the Rhine; it would make this chapter much too long. And to do it well, one should write like a god; and his style flow onward royally with breaks and dashes, like the waters of that royal river, and antique, quaint, and Gothic times, be reflected in it. Alas! this evening my style flows not at all. Flow, then, into this smoke-colored goblet, thou blood of the Rhine! out of thy prison-house,—out of thy long-necked, tapering flask, in shape not unlike a church-spire among thy native hills; and, from the crystal belfry, loud ring the merry tinkling bells, while I drink a health to my hero, in whose heart is sadness, and in whose ears the bells of Andernach are ringing noon.

He is threading his way alone through a narrow alley, and now up a flight of stone steps, and along the city wall, towards that old round tower, built by the Archbishop Frederick of Cologne in the twelfth century. It has a romantic interest in his eyes; for he has still in his mind and heart that beautiful sketch of Carové, in which is described a day on the tower of Andernach. He finds the old keeper and his wife still there; and the old keeper closes the door behind him slowly, as of old, lest he should jam too hard the poor souls in Purgatory, whose fate it is to suffer in the cracks of doors and hinges. But alas! alas! the daughter, the maiden with long, dark eyelashes! she is asleep in her little grave, under the linden trees of Feldkirche, with rosemary in her folded hands!

Flemming returned to the hotel disappointed. As he passed along the narrow streets, he was dreaming of many things; but mostly of the keeper's daughter, asleep in the churchyard of Feldkirche. Suddenly, on turning the corner of an ancient, gloomy church, his attention was arrested by a little chapel in an angle of the wall. It was only a small thatched roof, like a bird's nest; under which stood a rude wooden image of the Saviour on the Cross. A real crown of thorns was upon his head, which was bowed downward, as if in the death agony; and drops of blood were falling down his cheeks, and from his hands and feet and side. The face was haggard and ghastly beyond all expression; and wore a look of unutterable bodily anguish. The rude sculptor had given it this, but his art could go no farther. The sublimity of death in a dying Saviour, the expiring God-likeness of Jesus of Nazareth was not there. The artist had caught no heavenly inspiration from his theme. All was coarse, harsh, and revolting to a sensitive mind; and Flemming turned away with a shudder, as he saw this fearful image gazing at him, with its fixed and half-shut eyes.

He soon reached the hotel, but that face of agony still haunted him. He could not refrain from speaking of it to a very old woman, who sat knitting by the window of the dining-room, in a high-backed, old-fashioned arm-chair. I believe she was the innkeeper's grandmother. At all events she was old enough to be so. She took off her owl-eyed spectacles, and, as she wiped the glasses with her handkerchief, said;

"Thou dear Heaven! Is it possible! Did you never hear of the Christ of Andernach?"

Flemming answered in the negative.

"Thou dear Heaven!" continued the old woman. "It is a very wonderful story; and a true one, as every good Christian in Andernach will tell you. And it all happened before the death of my blessed man, four years ago, let me see,—yes, four years ago, come Christmas."

Here the old woman stopped speaking, but went on with her knitting. Other thoughts seemed to occupy her mind. She was thinking, no doubt, of her blessed man, as German widows call their dead husbands. But Flemming having expressed an ardent wish to hear the wonderful story, she told it, in nearly the following words.

"There was once a poor old woman in Andernach whose name was Frau Martha, and she lived all alone in a house by herself, and loved all the Saints and the blessed Virgin, and was as good as an angel, and sold pies down by the Rheinkrahn. But her house was very old, and the roof-tiles were broken, and she was too poor to get new ones, and the rain kept coming in, and no Christian soul in Andernach would help her. But the Frau Martha was a good woman, and never did anybody any harm, but went to mass every morning, and sold pies by the Rheinkrahn. Now one dark, windy night, when all the good Christians in Andernach were abed and asleep in the feathers, Frau Martha, who slept under the roof, heard a great noise over her head, and in her chamber, drip! drip! drip! as if the rain were dropping down through the broken tiles. Dear soul! and sure enough it was. And then there was a pounding and hammering overhead, as if somebody were at work on the roof; and she thought it was Pelz-Nickel tearing the tiles off, because she had not been to confession often enough. So she began to pray; and the faster she said her Pater-noster and her Ave-Maria, the faster Pelz-Nickel pounded and pulled; and drip! drip! drip! it went all round her in the dark chamber, till the poor woman was frightened out of her wits, and ran to the window to call for help. Then in a moment all was still,—death-still. But she saw a light streaming through the mist and rain, and a great shadow on the house opposite. And then somebody came down from the top of her house by a ladder, and had a lantern in his hand; and he took the ladder on his shoulder and went down the street. But she could not see clearly, because the window was streaked with rain. And in the morning the old broken tiles were found scattered about the street, and there were new ones on the roof, and the old house has never leaked to this blessed day.

"As soon as mass was over Frau Martha told the priest what had happened, and he said it was not Pelz-Nickel, but, without doubt, St. Castor or St. Florian. Then she went to the market and told Frau Bridget all about it; and Frau Bridget said, that, two nights before, Hans Claus, the cooper, had heard a great pounding in his shop, and in the morning found new hoops on all his old hogsheads; and that a man with a lantern and a ladder had been seen riding out of town at midnight on a donkey, and that the same night the old windmill, at Kloster St. Thomas, had been mended up, and the old gate of the churchyard at Feldkirche made as good as new, though nobody knew how the man got across the river. Then Frau Martha went down to the Rheinkrahn and told all these stories over again; and the old ferryman of Fahr said he could tell something about it; for, the very night that the churchyard-gate was mended, he was lying awake in his bed, because he could not sleep, and he heard a loud knocking at the door, and

somebody calling to him to get up and set him over the river. And when he got up, he saw a man down by the river with a lantern and a ladder; but as he was going down to him, the man blew out the light, and it was so dark he could not see who he was; and his boat was old and leaky, and he was afraid to set him over in the dark; but the man said he must be in Andernach that night; and so he set him over. And after they had crossed the river, he watched the man, till he came to an image of the Holy Virgin, and saw him put the ladder against the wall, and go up and light his lamp, and then walk along the street. And in the morning he found his old boat all caulked, and tight, and painted red, and he could not for his blessed life tell who did it, unless it were the man with the lantern. Dear soul! how strange it was!

"And so it went on for some time; and, whenever the man with the lantern had been seen walking through the street at night, so sure as the morning came, some work had been done for the sake of some good soul; and everybody knew he did it; and yet nobody could find out who he was, nor where he lived;—for, whenever they came near him, he blew out his light, and turned down another street, and, if they followed him, he suddenly disappeared, nobody could tell how. And some said it was Rübezahl; and some, Pelz-Nickel; and some, St. Anthony-on-the-Health.

"Now one stormy night a poor, sinful creature was wandering about the streets, with her babe in her arms, and she was hungry, and cold, and no soul in Andernach would take her in. And when she came to the church, where the great crucifix stands, she saw no light in the little chapel at the corner; but she sat down on a stone at the foot of the cross and began to pray, and prayed, till she fell asleep, with her poor little babe on her bosom. But she did not sleep long; for a bright light shone full in her face; and, when she opened her eyes, she saw a pale man, with a lantern, standing right before her. He was almost naked; and there was blood upon his hands and body, and great tears in his beautiful eyes, and his face was like the face of the Saviour on the cross. Not a single word did he say to the poor woman; but looked at her compassionately, and gave her a loaf of bread, and took the little babe in his arms, and kissed it. Then the mother looked up to the great crucifix, but there was no image there; and she shrieked and fell down as if she were dead. And there she was found with her child; and a few days after they both died, and were buried together in one grave. And nobody would have believed her story, if a woman, who lived at the corner, had not gone to the window, when she heard the scream, and seen the figure hang the lantern up in its place, and then set the ladder against the wall, and go up and nail itself to the cross. Since that night it has never moved again. Ach! Herr Je!"

Such was the legend of the Christ of Andernach, as the old woman in spectacles told it to Flemming. It made a painful impression on his sick and morbid soul; and he felt now for the first time in full force, how great is the power of popular superstition.

The post-chaise was now at the door, and Flemming was soon on the road to Coblentz, a city which stands upon the Rhine, at the mouth of the Mosel, opposite Ehrenbreitstein. It is by no means a long drive from Andernach to Coblentz; and the only incident which occurred to enliven the way was the appearance of a fat, red-faced man on horseback, trotting slowly towards Andernach. As they met, the mad little postilion gave him a friendly cut with his whip, and broke out into an exclamation, which showed he was from Münster;

"Jesmariosp! my friend! How is the Man in the Custom-House?"

Now to any candid mind this would seem a fair question enough; but not so thought the red-faced man on horseback; for he waxed exceedingly angry, and replied, as the chaise whirled by;

"The devil take you, and your Westphalian ham, and pumpernickel!"

Flemming called to his servant, and the servant to the postilion, for an explanation of this short dialogue; and the explanation was, that on the belfry of the Kaufhaus in Coblentz, is a huge head, with a brazen helmet and a beard; and whenever the clock strikes, at each stroke of the hammer, this giant's head opens its great jaws and smites its teeth together, as if, like the brazen head of Friar Bacon, it would say; "Time was; Time is; Time is past." This figure is known through all the country round about, as "The Man in the Custom-House"; and, when a friend in the country meets a friend from Coblentz, instead of saying, "How are all the good people in Coblentz?"—he says, "How is the Man in the Custom-House?" Thus the giant has a great part to play in the town; and thus ended the first day of Flemming's Rhine-journey; and the only good deed he had done was to give an alms to a poor beggar woman, who lifted up her trembling hands and exclaimed;

"Thou blessed babe!"

After all, a journey up the Rhine, in the mists and solitude of December, is not so unpleasant as the reader may perhaps imagine. You have the whole road and river to yourself. Nobody is on the wing; hardly a single traveller. The ruins are the same; and the river, and the outlines of the hills; and there are few living figures in the landscape to wake you from your musings, distract your thoughts, and cover you with dust.

Thus, likewise, thought our traveller, as he continued his journey on the morrow. The day is overcast, and the clouds threaten rain or snow. Why does he stop at the little village of Capellen? Because, right above him on the high cliff, the glorious ruin of Stolzenfels is looking at him with its hollow eyes, and beckoning to him with its gigantic finger, as if to say; "Come up hither, and I will tell thee an old tale." Therefore he alights, and goes up the narrow village lane, and up the stone steps, and up the steep pathway, and throws himself into the arms of that ancient ruin, and holds his breath, to hear the quick footsteps of the falling snow, like the footsteps of angels descending upon earth. And that ancient ruin speaks to him with its hollow voice, and says;

"Beware of dreams! Beware of the illusions of fancy! Beware of the solemn deceivings of thy vast desires! Beneath me flows the Rhine, and, like the stream of Time, it flows amid the ruins of the Past. I see myself therein, and I know that I am old. Thou, too, shalt be old. Be wise in season. Like the stream of thy life, runs the stream beneath us. Down from the distant Alps,—out into the wide world, it bursts away, like a youth from the house of his fathers. Broad-breasted and strong, and with earnest endeavours, like manhood, it makes itself a way through these difficult mountain passes. And at length, in its old age, its stops, and its steps are weary and slow, and it sinks into the sand, and, through its grave, passes into the great ocean, which is its eternity. Thus shall it be with thee.

"In ancient times there dwelt within these halls a follower of Jesus of Jerusalem,—an Archbishop in the church of Christ. He gave himself up to dreams; to the illusions of fancy; to the vast desires of the human soul. He sought after the impossible. He sought after the Elixir of Life,—the Philosopher's Stone. The wealth, that should have fed the poor, was melted in his crucibles. Within these walls the Eagle of the clouds sucked the blood of the Red Lion, and received the spiritual Love of the Green Dragon, but alas! was childless. In solitude and utter silence did the disciple of the Hermetic Philosophy toil from day to day, from night to night. From the place where thou standest, he gazed at evening upon hills, and vales, and waters spread beneath him; and saw how the setting sun had changed them all to gold, by an alchymy more cunning than his own. He saw the world beneath his feet; and said in his heart, that he

alone was wise. Alas! he read more willingly in the book of Paracelsus, than in the book of Nature; and, believing that `where reason hath experience, faith hath no mind,' would fain have made unto himself a child, not as Nature teaches us, but as the Philosopher taught,—a poor homunculus, in a glass bottle. And he died poor and childless!"

Whether it were worth while to climb the Stolzenfels to hear such a homily as this, some persons may perhaps doubt. But Paul Flemming doubted not. He laid the lesson to heart; and it would have saved him many an hour of sorrow, if he had learned that lesson better, and remembered it longer.

In ancient times, there stood in the citadel of Athens three statues of Minerva. The first was of olive wood, and, according to popular tradition, had fallen from heaven. The second was of bronze, commemorating the victory of Marathon; and the third of gold and ivory,—a great miracle of art, in the age of Pericles. And thus in the citadel of Time stands Man himself. In childhood, shaped of soft and delicate wood, just fallen from heaven; in manhood, a statue of bronze, commemorating struggle and victory; and lastly, in the maturity of age, perfectly shaped in gold and ivory,—a miracle of art!

Flemming had already lived through the olive age. He was passing into the age of bronze, into his early manhood; and in his hands the flowers of Paradise were changing to the sword and shield.

And this reminds me, that I have not yet described my hero. I will do it now, as he stands looking down on the glorious landscape;—but in few words. Both in person and character he resembled Harold, the Fair-Hair of Norway, who is described, in the old Icelandic Death-Song of Regner Hairy-Breeches, as "the young chief so proud of his flowing locks; he who spent his mornings among the young maidens; he who loved to converse with the handsome widows." This was an amiable weakness; and it sometimes led him into mischief. Imagination was the ruling power of his mind. His thoughts were twin-born; the thought itself, and its figurative semblance in the outer world. Thus, through the quiet, still waters of his soul each image floated double, "swan and shadow."

These traits of character, a good heart and a poetic imagination, made his life joyous and the world beautiful; till at length Death cut down the sweet, blue flower, that bloomed beside him, and wounded him with that sharp sickle, so that he bowed his head, and would fain have been bound up in the same sheaf with the sweet, blue flower. Then the world seemed to him less beautiful, and life became earnest. It would have been well if he could have forgotten the past; that he might not so mournfully have lived in it, but might have enjoyed and improved the present. But this his heart refused to do; and ever, as he floated upon the great sea of life, he looked down through the transparent waters, checkered with sunshine and shade, into the vast chambers of the mighty deep, in which his happier days had sunk, and wherein they were lying still visible, like golden sands, and precious stones, and pearls; and, half in despair, half in hope, he grasped downward after them again, and drew back his hand, filled only with seaweed, and dripping with briny tears!—And between him and those golden sands, a radiant image floated, like the spirit in Dante's Paradise, singing "Ave-Maria!" and while it sang, down-sinking, and slowly vanishing away.

The truth is, that in all things he acted more from impulse than from fixed principle; as is the case with most young men. Indeed, his principles hardly had time to take root; for he pulled them all up, every now and then, as children do the flowers they have planted,—to see if they are growing. Yet there was much in him which was good; for underneath the flowers and green-sward of poetry, and the good principles which would have taken root, had he given them time, therelay a strong and healthy soil of

common sense,—freshened by living springs of feeling, and enriched by many faded hopes, that had fallen upon it like dead leaves.

CHAPTER IV
THE LANDLADY'S DAUGHTER

"Allez Fuchs! allez lustig!" cried the impatient postilion to his horses, in accents, which, like the wild echo of the Lurley Felsen, came first from one side of the river, and then from the other,—that is to say, in words alternately French and German. The truth is, he was tired of waiting; and when Flemming had at length resumed his seat in the post-chaise, the poor horses had to make up the time lost in dreams on the mountain. This is far oftener the case, than most people imagine. One half of the world has to sweat and groan, that the other half may dream. It would have been a difficult task for the traveller or his postilion to persuade the horses, that these dreams were all for their good.

The next stopping-place was the little tavern of the Star, an out-of-the-way corner in the town of Salzig. It stands on the banks of the Rhine; and, directly in front of it, sheer from the water's edge, rise the mountains of Liebenstein and Sternenfels, each with its ruined castle. These are the Brothers of the old tradition, still gazing at each other face to face; and beneath them in the valley stands a cloister,—meek emblem of that orphan child, they both so passionately loved.

In a small, flat-bottomed boat did the landlady's daughter row Flemming "over the Rhine-stream, rapid and roaring wide." She was a beautiful girl of sixteen; with black hair, and dark, lovely eyes, and a face that had a story to tell. How different faces are in this particular! Some of them speak not. They are books in which not a line is written, save perhaps a date. Others are great family bibles, with all the Old and New Testament written in them. Others are Mother Goose and nursery tales;—others bad tragedies or pickle-herring farces; and others, like that of the landlady's daughter at the Star, sweet love-anthologies, and songs of the affections. It was on that account, that Flemming said to her, as they glided out into the swift stream;

"My dear child! do you know the story of the Liebenstein?"

"The story of the Liebenstein," she answered, "I got by heart, when I was a little child."

And here her large, dark, passionate eyes looked into Flemming's, and he doubted not, that she had learned the story far too soon, and far too well. That story he longed to hear, as if it were unknown to him; for he knew that the girl, who had got it by heart when a child, would tell it as it should be told. So he begged her to repeat the story, which she was but too glad to do; for she loved and believed it, as if it had all been written in the Bible. But before she began, she rested a moment on her oars, and taking the crucifix, which hung suspended from her neck, kissed it, and then let it sink down into her bosom, as if it were an anchor she was letting down into her heart. Meanwhile her moist, dark eyes were turned to heaven. Perhaps her soul was walking with the souls of Cunizza, and Rahab, and Mary Magdalen. Or perhaps she was thinking of that Nun, of whom St. Gregory says, in his Dialogues, that, having greedily eaten a lettuce in a garden, without making the sign of the cross, she found herself soon after possessed with a devil.

The probability, however, is, that she was looking up to the ruined castles only, and not to heaven, for she soon began her story, and told Flemming how, a great, great many years ago, an old man lived in the Liebenstein with his two sons; and how both the young men loved the Lady Geraldine, an orphan, under their father's care; and how the elder brother went away in despair, and the younger was betrothed to the Lady Geraldine; and how they were as happy as Aschenputtel and the Prince. And then the holy Saint Bernard came and carried away all the young men to the war, just as Napoleon did afterwards; and the young lord went to the Holy Land, and the Lady Geraldine sat in her tower and wept, and waited for her lover's return, while the old father built the Sternenfels for them to live in when they were married. And when it was finished, the old man died; and the elder brother came back and lived in the Liebenstein, and took care of the gentle Lady. Ere long there came news from the Holy Land, that the war was over; and the heart of the gentle Lady beat with joy, till she heard that her faithless lover was coming back with a Greek wife,—the wicked man! and then she went into a convent and became a holy nun. So the young lord of Sternenfels came home, and lived in his castle in great splendor with the Greek woman, who was a wicked woman, and did what she ought not to do. But the elder brother was angry for the wrong done the gentle Lady, and challenged the lord of Sternenfels to single combat. And, while they were fighting with their great swords in the valley of Bornhofen behind the castle, the convent bells began to ring, and the Lady Geraldine came forth with a train of nuns all dressed in white, and made the brothers friends again, and told them she was the bride of Heaven, and happier in her convent than she could have been in the Liebenstein or the Sternenfels. And when the brothers returned, they found that the false Greek wife had gone away with another knight. So they lived together in peace, and were never married. And when they died—"

"Lisbeth! Lisbeth!" cried a sharp voice from the shore, "Lisbeth! Where are you taking the gentleman?"

This recalled the poor girl to her senses; and she saw how fast they were floating down stream. For in telling the story she had forgotten every thing else, and the swift current had swept them down to the tall walnut trees of Kamp. They landed in front of the Capucin Monastery. Lisbeth led the way through the little village, and turning to the right pointed up the romantic, lonely valley which leads to the Liebenstein, and even offered to go up. But Flemming patted her cheek and shook his head. He went up the valley alone.

CHAPTER V

JEAN PAUL, THE ONLY-ONE

The man in the play, who wished for `some forty pounds of lovely beef, placed in a Mediterranean sea of brewis,' might have seen his ample desires almost realized at the table d'hôte of the Rheinischen Hof, in Mayence, where Flemming dined that day. At the head of the table sat a gentleman, with a smooth, broad forehead, and large, intelligent eyes. He was from Baireuth in Franconia; and talked about poetry and Jean Paul, to a pale, romantic-looking lady on his right. There was music all dinner-time, at the other end of the hall; a harp and a horn and a voice; so that a great part of the fat gentleman's conversation with the pale lady was lost to Flemming, who sat opposite to her, and could look right into her large, melancholy eyes. But what he heard, so much interested him,—indeed, the very name of the beloved Jean Paul would have been enough for this,—that he ventured to join in the conversation, and asked the German if he had known the poet personally.

"Yes; I knew him well," replied the stranger. "I am a native of Baireuth, where he passed the best years of his life. In my mind the man and the author are closely united. I never read a page of his writings without hearing his voice, and seeing his form before me. There he sits, with his majestic, mountainous forehead, his mild blue eyes, and finely cut nose and mouth; his massive frame clad loosely and carelessly in an old green frock, from the pockets of which the corners of books project, and perhaps the end of a loaf of bread, and the nose of a bottle;—a straw hat, lined with green, lying near him; a huge walking-stick in his hand, and at his feet a white poodle, with pink eyes and a string round his neck. You would sooner have taken him for a master-carpenter than for a poet. Is he a favorite author of yours?"

Flemming answered in the affirmative.

"But a foreigner must find it exceedingly difficult to understand him," said the gentleman. "It is by no means an easy task for us Germans."

"I have always observed," replied Flemming, "that the true understanding and appreciation of a poet depend more upon individual, than upon national character. If there be a sympathy between the minds of writer and reader, the bounds and barriers of a foreign tongue are soon overleaped. If you once understand an author's character, the comprehension of his writings becomes easy."

"Very true," replied the German, "and the character of Richter is too marked to be easily misunderstood. Its prominent traits are tenderness and manliness,—qualities, which are seldom found united in so high a degree as in him. Over all he sees, over all he writes, are spread the sunbeams of a cheerful spirit,— the light of inexhaustible human love. Every sound of human joy and of human sorrow finds a deep-resounding echo in his bosom. In every man, he loves his humanity only, not his superiority. The avowed object of all his literary labors was to raise up again the down-sunken faith in God, virtue, and immortality; and, in an egotistical, revolutionary age, to warm again our human sympathies, which have now grown cold. And not less boundless is his love for nature,—for this outward, beautiful world. He embraces it all in his arms."

"Yes," answered Flemming, almost taking the words out of the stranger's mouth, "for in his mind all things become idealized. He seems to describe himself when he describes the hero of his Titan, as a child, rocking in a high wind upon the branches of a full-blossomed apple-tree, and, as its summit, blown abroad by the wind, now sunk him in deep green, and now tossed him aloft in deep blue and glancing sunshine,—in his imagination stood that tree gigantic;—it grew alone in the universe, as if it were the tree of eternal life; its roots struck down into the abyss; the white and red clouds hung as blossoms upon it; the moon asfruit; the little stars sparkled like dew, and Albano reposed in its measureless summit; and a storm swayed the summit out of Day into Night, and out of Night into Day."

"Yet the spirit of love," interrupted the Franconian, "was not weakness, but strength. It was united in him with great manliness. The sword of his spirit had been forged and beaten by poverty. Its temper had been tried by a thirty years' war. It was not broken, not even blunted; but rather strengthened and sharpened by the blows it gave and received. And, possessing this noble spirit of humanity, endurance, and self-denial, he made literature his profession; as if he had been divinely commissioned to write. He seems to have cared for nothing else, to have thought of nothing else, than living quietly and making books. He says, that he felt it his duty, not to enjoy, nor to acquire, but to write; and boasted, that he had made as many books as he had lived years."

"And what do you Germans consider the prominent characteristics of his genius?"

"Most undoubtedly his wild imagination and his playfulness. He throws over all things a strange and magic coloring. You are startled at the boldness and beauty of his figures and illustrations, which are scattered everywhere with a reckless prodigality;—multitudinous, like the blossoms of early summer,—and as fragrant and beautiful. With a thousand extravagances are mingled ten thousand beauties of thought and expression, which kindle the reader's imagination, and lead it onward in a bold flight, through the glow of sunrise and sunset, and the dewy coldness and starlight of summer nights. He is difficult to understand,—intricate,— strange,—drawing his illustrations from every by-corner of science, art, and nature,—a comet, among the bright stars of German literature. When you read his works, it is as if you were climbing a high mountain, in merry company, to see the sun rise. At times you are enveloped in mist,—the morning wind sweeps by you with a shout,—you hear the far-off muttering thunders. Wide beneath you spreads the landscape,—field, meadow, town, and winding river. The ringing of distant church-bells, or the sound of solemn village clock, reaches you;—then arises the sweet and manifold fragrance of flowers,—the birds begin to sing,—the vapors roll away,—up comes the glorious sun,—you revel like the lark in the sunshine and bright blue heaven, and all is a delirious dream of soul and sense,—when suddenly a friend at your elbow laughs aloud, and offers you a piece of Bologna sausage. As in real life, so in his writings,—the serious and the comic, the sublime and the grotesque, the pathetic and the ludicrous are mingled together. At times he is sententious, energetic, simple; then again, obscure and diffuse. His thoughts are like mummies embalmed in spices, and wrapped about with curious envelopements; but within these the thoughts themselves are kings. At times glad, beautiful images, airy forms, move by you, graceful, harmonious;—at times the glaring, wild-looking fancies, chained together by hyphens, brackets, and dashes, brave and base, high and low, all in their motley dresses, go sweeping down the dusty page, like the galley-slaves, that sweep the streets of Rome, where you may chance to see the nobleman and the peasant manacled together."

Flemming smiled at the German's warmth, to which the presence of the lady, and the Laubenheimer wine, seemed each to have contributed something, and then said;

"Better an outlaw, than not free!—These are his own words. And thus he changes at his will. Like the God Thor, of the old Northern mythology, he now holds forth the seven bright stars in the bright heaven above us, and now hides himself in clouds, and pounds away with his great hammer."

"And yet this is not affectation in him," rejoined the German. "It is his nature, it is Jean Paul. And the figures and ornaments of his style, wild, fantastic, and oft-times startling, like those in Gothic cathedrals, are not merely what they seem, but massive coignes and buttresses, which support the fabric. Remove them, and the roof and walls fall in. And through these gurgoyles, these wild faces, carved upon spouts and gutters, flow out, like gathered rain, the bright, abundant thoughts, that have fallen from heaven.

"And all he does, is done with a kind of serious playfulness. He is a sea-monster, disporting himself on the broad ocean; his very sport is earnest; there is something majestic and serious about it. In every thing there is strength, a rough good-nature, all sunshine overhead, and underneath the heavy moaning of the sea. Well may he be called 'Jean Paul, the Only-One.'"

With such discourse the hour of dinner passed; and after dinner Flemming went to the Cathedral. They were singing vespers. A beadle, dressed in blue, with a cocked hat, and a crimson sash and collar, was strutting, like a turkey, along the aisles. This important gentleman conducted Flemming through the church, and showed him the choir, with its heavy-sculptured stalls of oak, and the beautiful figures in brown stone, over the bishops' tombs. He then led him, by a side-door, into the old and ruined cloisters

of St. Willigis. Through the low gothic arches the sunshine streamed upon the pavement of tombstones, whose images and inscriptions are mostly effaced by the footsteps of many generations. There stands the tomb of Frauenlob, the Minnesinger. His face is sculptured on an entablature in the wall; a fine, strongly-marked, and serious countenance. Below it is a bas-relief, representing the poet's funeral. He is carried to his grave by ladies, whose praise he sang, and thereby won the name of Frauenlob.

"This then," said Flemming, "is the grave, not of Praise-God Bare-bones, but of Praise-the-Ladies Meissen, who wrote songs `somewhat of lust, and somewhat of love.' But where sleeps the dust of his rival and foe, sweet Master Bartholomew Rainbow?"

He meant this for an aside; but the turkey-cock picked it up and answered;

"I do not know. He did not belong to this parish."

It was already night, when Flemming crossed the Roman bridge over the Nahe, and entered the town of Bingen. He stopped at the White Horse; and, before going to bed, looked out into the dim starlight from his window towards the Rhine, and his heart leaped up to behold the bold outline of the neighbouring hills crested with Gothic ruins;—which in the morning proved to be only a high, slated roof with fantastic chimneys.

The morning was bright and frosty; and the river tinged with gay colors from the rising sun. A soft, thin vapor floated in the air. In the sunbeams flashed the hoar-frost, like silver stars; and through a long avenue of trees, whose dripping branches bent and scattered pearls before him, Paul Flemming journeyed on in triumph.

I will not prolong this journey, for I am weary and way-worn, and would fain be at Heidelberg with my readers, and my hero. It was already night when he reached the Manheim gate, and drove down the long Hauptstrasse so slowly, that it seemed to him endless. The shops were lighted on each side of the street, and he saw faces at the windows here and there, and figures passing in the lamp-light, visible for a moment and then swallowed up in the darkness. The thoughts that filled his mind were strange; as are always the thoughts of a traveller, who enters for the first time a strange city. This little world had been going on for centuries before he came; and would go on for centuries after he was gone. Of all the thousands who inhabited it he knew nothing; and what knew they, or thought, of the stranger, who, in that close post-chaise, weary with travel, and chilled by the evening wind, was slowly rumbling over the paved street! Truly, this world can go on without us, if we would but think so. If it had been a hearse instead of a post-chaise, it would have been all the same to the people of Heidelberg,—though by no means the same to Paul Flemming.

But at the farther end of the city, near the Castle and the Carls-Thor, one warm heart was waiting to receive him; and this was the German heart of his friend, the Baron of Hohenfels, with whom he was to pass the winter in Heidelberg. No sooner had the carriage stopped at the iron grated gate, and the postilion blown his horn, to announce the arrival of a traveller, than the Baron was seen among the servants at the door; and, a few moments afterwards, the two long-absent friends were in each other's arms, and Flemming received a kiss upon each cheek, and another on the mouth, as the pledge and seal of the German's friendship. They held each other long by the hand, and looked into each other's faces, and saw themselves in each other's eyes, both literally and figuratively; literally, inasmuch as the images were there; and figuratively, inasmuch as each was imagining what the other thought of him, after the lapse of some years. In friendly hopes and questionings and answers, the evening glided away at the

supper-table, where many more things were discussed than the roasted hare, and the Johannisberger; and they sat late into the night, conversing of the thoughts and feelings and delights, which fill the hearts of young men, who have already enjoyed and suffered, and hoped and been disappointed.

CHAPTER VI

HEIDELBERG AND THE BARON

High and hoar on the forehead of the Jettenbühl stands the Castle of Heidelberg. Behind it rise the oak-crested hills of the Geissberg and the Kaiserstuhl; and in front, from the broad terrace of masonry, you can almost throw a stone upon the roofs of the city, so close do they lie beneath. Above this terrace rises the broad front of the chapel of Saint Udalrich. On the left, stands the slender octagon tower of the horologe, and, on the right, a huge round tower, battered and shattered by the mace of war, shores up with its broad shoulders the beautiful palace and garden-terrace of Elisabeth, wife of the Pfalzgraf Frederick. In the rear are older palaces and towers, forming a vast, irregular quadrangle;—Rodolph's ancient castle, with its Gothic gloriette and fantastic gables; the Giant's Tower, guarding the drawbridge over the moat; the Rent Tower, with the linden-trees growing on its summit, and the magnificent Rittersaal of Otho-Henry, Count Palatine of the Rhine and grand seneschal of the Holy Roman Empire. From the gardens behind the castle, you pass under the archway of the Giant's Tower into the great court-yard. The diverse architecture of different ages strikes the eye; and curious sculptures. In niches on the wall of Saint Udalrich's chapel stand rows of knights in armour, all broken and dismembered; and on the front of Otho's Rittersaal, the heroes of Jewish history and classic fable. You enter the open and desolate chambers of the ruin; and on every side are medallions and family arms; the Globe of the Empire and the Golden Fleece, or the Eagle of the Cæsars, resting on the escutcheons of Bavaria and the Palatinate. Over the windows and door-ways and chimney-pieces, are sculptures and mouldings of exquisite workmanship; and the eye is bewildered by the profusion of caryatides, and arabesques, and rosettes, and fan-like flutings, and garlands of fruits and flowers and acorns, and bullocks'-heads with draperies of foliage, and muzzles of lions, holding rings in their teeth. The cunning hand of Art was busy for six centuries, in raising and adorning these walls; the mailed hands of Time and War have defaced and overthrown them in less than two. Next to the Alhambra of Granada, the Castle of Heidelberg is the most magnificent ruin of the Middle Ages.

In the valley below flows the rushing stream of the Neckar. Close from its margin, on the opposite side, rises the Mountain of All Saints, crowned with the ruins of a convent; and up the valley stretches the mountain-curtain of the Odenwald. So close and many are the hills, which eastward shut the valley in, that the river seems a lake. But westward it opens, upon the broad plain of the Rhine, like the mouth of a trumpet; and like the blast of a trumpet is at times the wintry wind through this narrow mountain pass. The blue Alsatian hills rise beyond; and, on a platform or strip of level land, between the Neckar and the mountains, right under the castle, stands the city of Heidelberg; as the old song says, "a pleasant city, when it has done raining."

Something of this did Paul Flemming behold, when he rose the next morning and looked from his window. It was a warm, vapory morning, and a struggle was going on between the mist and the rising sun. The sun had taken the hill-tops, but the mist still kept possession of the valley and the town. The steeple of the great church rose through a dense mass of snow-white clouds; and eastward, on the hills, the dim vapors were rolling across the windows of the ruined castle, like the fiery smoke of a great

conflagration. It seemed to him an image of the rising of the sun of Truth on a benighted world; its light streamed through the ruins of centuries; and, down in the valley of Time, the cross on the Christian church caught its rays, though the priests were singing in mist and darkness below.

In the warm breakfast-parlour he found the Baron, waiting for him. He was lying upon a sofa, in morning gown and purple-velvet slippers, both with flowers upon them. He had a guitar in his hand, and a pipe in his mouth, at the same time smoking, playing, and humming his favorite song from Goethe;

"The water rushed, the water swelled,

A fisher sat thereby."

Flemming could hardly refrain from laughing at the sight of his friend; and told him it reminded him of a street-musician he once saw in Aix-la-Chapelle, who was playing upon six instruments at once; having a helmet with bells on his head, a Pan's-reed in his cravat, a fiddle in his hand, a triangle on his knee, cymbals on his heels, and on his back a bass-drum, which he played with his elbows. To tell the truth, the Baron of Hohenfels was rather a miscellaneous youth, rather a universal genius. He pursued all things with eagerness, but for a short time only; music, poetry, painting, pleasure, even the study of the Pandects. His feelings were keenly alive to the enjoyment of life. His great defect was, that he was too much in love with human nature. But by the power of imagination, in him, the bearded goat was changed to a bright Capricornus:—no longer an animal on earth, but a constellation in heaven. An easy and indolent disposition made him gentle and childlike in his manners; and, in short, the beauty of his character, like that of the precious opal, was owing to a defect in its organization. His person was tall and slightly built; his hair light; and his eyes blue, and as beautiful as those of a girl. In the tones of his voice, there was something indescribably gentle and winning; and he spoke the German language, with the soft, musical accent of his native province of Curland. In his manners, if he had not `Antinous' easy sway,' he had at least an easy sway of his own. Such, in few words, was the bosom friend of Flemming.

"And what do you think of Heidelberg and the old castle up there?" said he, as they seated themselves at the breakfast-table.

"Last night the town seemed very long to me," replied Flemming; "and as to the castle, I have as yet had but a glimpse of it through the mist. They tell me there is nothing finer in its way, excepting the Alhambra of Granada; and no doubt I shall find it so. Only I wish the stone were gray and not red. But, red or gray, I foresee that I shall waste many a long hour in its desolate halls. Pray, does anybody live up there now-a-days?"

"Nobody," answered the Baron, "but the man, who shows the Heidelberg Ton, and Monsieur Charles de Grainberg, a Frenchman, who has been there sketching ever since the year eighteen-hundred and ten. He has, moreover, written a super-magnificent description of the ruin, in which he says, that during the day only birds of prey disturb it with their piercing cries, and at night, screech-owls, and other fallow deer. These are his own words. You must buy his book and his sketches."

"Yes, the quotation and the tone of your voice will certainly persuade me so to do."

"Take his or none, my friend, for you will find no others. And seriously, his sketches are very good. There is one on the wall there, which is beautiful, save and except that straddle-bug figure among the bushes in the corner."

"But is there no ghost, no haunted chamber in the old castle?" asked Flemming, after casting a hasty glance at the picture.

"Oh, certainly," replied the Baron; "there are two. There is the ghost of the Virgin Mary in Ruprecht's Tower, and the Devil in the Dungeon."

"Ha! that is grand!" exclaimed Flemming, with evident delight. "Tell me the whole story, quickly! I am as curious as a child."

"It is a tale of the times of Louis the Debonnaire," said the Baron, with a smile; "a mouldy tradition of a credulous age. His brother Frederick lived here in the castle with him, and had a flirtation with Leonore von Luzelstein, a lady of the court, whom he afterwards despised, and was consequently most cordially hated by her. From political motives he was equally hateful to certain petty German tyrants, who, in order to effect his ruin, accused him of heresy. But his brother Louis would not deliver him up to their fury, and they resolved to effect by stratagem, what they could not by intrigue. Accordingly, Leonore von Luzelstein, disguised as the Virgin Mary, and the father confessor of the Elector, in the costume of Satan, made their appearance in the Elector's bed-chamber at midnight, and frightened him so horribly, that he consented to deliver up his brother into the hands of two Black Knights, who pretended to be ambassadors from the Vehm-Gericht. They proceeded together to Frederick's chamber; where luckily old Gemmingen, a brave soldier, kept guard behind the arras. The monk went foremost in his Satanic garb; but, no sooner had he set foot in the prince's bed-chamber, than the brave Gemmingen drew his sword, and said quaintly, `Die, wretch!' and so he died. The rest took to their heels, and were heard of no more. And now the souls of Leonore and the monk haunt the scene of their midnight crime. You will find the story in Grainberg's book, worked up with a kind of red-morocco and burnt-cork sublimity, and great melo-dramatic clanking of chains, and hooting of owls, and other fallow deer!"

"After breakfast," said Flemming, "we will go up to the castle. I must get acquainted with this mirror of owls, this modern Till Eulenspiegel. See what a glorious morning we have! It is truly a wondrous winter! what summer sunshine; what soft Venetian fogs! How the wanton, treacherous air coquets with the old gray-beard trees! Such weather makes the grass and our beards grow apace! But we have an old saying in English, that winter never rots in the sky. So he will come down at last in his old-fashioned, mealy coat. We shall have snow in spring; and the blossoms will be all snow-flakes. And afterwards a summer, which will be no summer, but, as Jean Paul says, only a winter painted green. Is it not so?"

"Unless I am much deceived in the climate of Heidelberg," replied the Baron, "we shall not have to wait long for snow. We have sudden changes here, and I should not marvel much if it snowed before night."

"The greater reason for making good use of the morning sunshine, then. Let us hasten to the castle, after which my heart yearns."

CHAPTER VII

LIVES OF SCHOLARS

The forebodings of the Baron proved true. In the afternoon the weather changed. The western wind began to blow, and its breath drew a cloud-veil over the face of heaven, as a breath does over the human face in a mirror. Soon the snow began to fall. Athwart the distant landscape it swept like a white mist. The storm-wind came from the Alsatian hills, and struck the dense clouds aslant through the air. And ever faster fell the snow, a roaring torrent from those mountainous clouds. The setting sun glared wildly from the summit of the hills, and sank like a burning ship at sea, wrecked in the tempest. Thus the evening set in; and winter stood at the gate wagging his white and shaggy beard, like an old harper, chanting an old rhyme:—"How cold it is! how cold it is!"

"I like such a storm as this," said Flemming, who stood at the window, looking out into the tempest and the gathering darkness. "The silent falling of snow is to me one of the most solemn things in nature. The fall of autumnal leaves does not so much affect me. But the driving storm is grand. It startles me; it awakens me. It is wild and woful, like my own soul. I cannot help thinking of the sea; how the waves run and toss their arms about,—and the wind plays on those great harps, made by the shrouds and masts of ships. Winter is here in earnest! Whew! How the old churl whistles and threshes the snow! Sleet and rain are falling too. Already the trees are bearded with icicles; and the two broad branches of yonder pine look like the white mustache of some old German Baron."

"And to-morrow it will look more wintry still," said his friend. "We shall wake up and find that the frost-spirit has been at work all night building Gothic Cathedrals on our windows, just as the devil built the Cathedral of Cologne. So draw the curtains, and come sit here by the warm fire."

"And now," said Flemming, having done as his friend desired, "tell me something of Heidelberg and its University. I suppose we shall lead about as solitary and studious a life here as we did of yore in little Göttingen, with nothing to amuse us, save our own day-dreams."

"Pretty much so," replied the Baron; "which cannot fail to please you, since you are in pursuit of tranquillity. As to the University, it is, as you know, one of the oldest in Germany. It was founded in the fourteenth century by the Count Palatine Ruprecht, and had in the first year more than five hundred students, all busily committing to memory, after the old scholastic wise, the rules of grammar versified by Alexander de Villa Dei, and the extracts made by Peter the Spaniard from Michel Psellus's Synopsis of Aristotle's Organon, and the Categories, with Porphory's Commentaries. Truly, I do not much wonder, that Eregina Scotus should have been put to death by his scholars with their penknives. They must have been pushed to the very verge of despair."

"What a strange picture a University presents to the imagination. The lives of scholars in their cloistered stillness;—literary men of retired habits, and Professors who study sixteen hours a day, and never see the world but on a Sunday. Nature has, no doubt, for some wise purpose, placed in their hearts this love of literary labor and seclusion. Otherwise, who would feed the undying lamp of thought? But for such men as these, a blast of wind through the chinks and crannies of this old world, or the flapping of a conqueror's banner, would blow it out forever. The light of the soul is easily extinguished. And whenever I reflect upon these things I become aware of the great importance, in a nation's history, of the individual fame of scholars and literary men. I fear, that it is far greater than the world is willing to acknowledge; or, perhaps I should say, than the world has thought of acknowledging. Blot out from England's history the names of Chaucer, Shakspere, Spenser, and Milton only, and how much of her glory would you blot out with them! Take from Italy such names as Dante, Petrarch, Boccaccio, Michel Angelo, and Raphael, and how much would still be wanting to the completeness of her glory! How would the history of Spain look if the leaves were torn out, on which are written the names of

Cervantes, Lope de Vega, and Calderon! What would be the fame of Portugal, without her Camoens; of France, without her Racine, and Rabelais, and Voltaire; or Germany, without her Martin Luther, her Goethe, and Schiller!—Nay, what were the nations of old, without their philosophers, poets, and historians! Tell me, do not these men in all ages and in all places, emblazon with bright colors the armorial bearings of their country? Yes, and far more than this; for in all ages and all places they give humanity assurance of its greatness; and say; Call not this time or people wholly barbarous; for thus much, even then and there, could the human mind achieve! But the boisterous world has hardly thought of acknowledging all this. Therein it has shown itself somewhat ungrateful. Else, whence the great reproach, the general scorn, the loud derision, with which, to take a familiar example, the monks of the Middle Ages are regarded! That they slept their lives away is most untrue. For in an age when books were few,—so few, so precious, that they were often chained to their oaken shelves with iron chains, like galley-slaves to their benches, these men, with their laborious hands, copied upon parchment all the lore and wisdom of the past, and transmitted it to us. Perhaps it is not too much to say, that, but for these monks, not one line of the classics would have reached our day. Surely, then, we can pardon something to those superstitious ages, perhaps even the mysticism of the scholastic philosophy, since, after all, we can find no harm in it, only the mistaking of the possible for the real, and the high aspirings of the human mind after a long-sought and unknown somewhat. I think the name of Martin Luther, the monk of Wittemberg, alone sufficient to redeem all monkhood from the reproach of laziness! If this will not, perhaps the vast folios of Thomas Aquinas will;—or the countless manuscripts, still treasured in old libraries, whose yellow and wrinkled pages remind one of the hands that wrote them, and the faces that once bent over them."

"An eloquent homily," said the Baron laughing, "a most touching appeal in behalf of suffering humanity! For my part, I am no friend of this entire seclusion from the world. It has a very injurious effect on the mind of a scholar. The Chinese proverb is true; a single conversation across the table with a wise man, is better than ten years' mere study of books. I have known some of these literary men, who thus shut themselves up from the world. Their minds never come in contact with those of their fellow-men. They read little. They think much. They are mere dreamers. They know not what is new nor what is old. They often strike upon trains of thought, which stand written in good authors some century or so back, and are even current in the mouths of men around them. But they know it not; and imagine they are bringing forward something very original, when they publish their thoughts."

"It reminds me," replied Flemming, "of what Dr. Johnson said of Goldsmith, when he proposed to travel abroad in order to bring home improvements;—'He will bring home a wheelbarrow, and call that an improvement.' It is unfortunately the same with some of these scholars."

"And the worst of it is," said the Baron, "that, in solitude, some fixed idea will often take root in the mind, and grow till it overshadow all one's thoughts. To this must all opinions come; no thought can enter there, which shall not be wedded to the fixed idea. There it remains, and grows. It is like the watchman's wife, in the tower of Waiblingen, who grew to such a size, that she could not get down the narrow stair-case; and, when her husband died, his successor was forced to marry the fat widow in the tower."

"I remember an old English comedy," said Flemming laughing, "in which a scholar is described, as a creature, that can strike fire in the morning at his tinder-box,—put on a pair of lined slippers,—sit ruminating till dinner, and then go to his meat when the bell rings;—one that hath a peculiar gift in a cough, and a license to spit;—or, if you will have him defined by negatives, he is one that cannot make a good leg;—one that cannot eat a mess of broth cleanly. What think you of that?"

"That it is just as people are always represented in English comedy," said the Baron. "The portrait is over-charged,—caricatured."

"And yet," continued Flemming, "no longer ago than yesterday, in the Preface of a work by Dr. Rosenkranz, Professor of Philosophy in the University of Halle, I read this passage."

He opened a book and read.

"Here in Halle, where we have no public garden and no Tivoli, no London Exchange, no Paris Chamber of Deputies, no Berlin nor Vienna Theatres, no Strassburg Minster, nor Salzburg Alps,—no Grecian ruins nor fantastic Catholicism, in fine, nothing, which after one's daily task is finished, can divert and refresh him, without his knowing or caring how,—I consider the sight of a proof-sheet quite as delightful as a walk in the Prater of Vienna. I fill my pipe very quietly, take out my ink-stand and pens, seat myself in the corner of my sofa, read, correct, and now for the first time really set about thinking what I have written. To see this origin of a book, this metamorphosis of manuscript into print, is a delight to which I give myself up entirely. Look you, this melancholy pleasure, which would have furnished the departed Voss with worthy matter for more than one blessed Idyl—(the more so, as on such occasions, I am generally arrayed in a morning gown, though I am sorry to say, not a calamanco one, with great flowers;) this melancholy pleasure was already grown here in Halle to a sweet, pedantic habit. Since I began my hermit's life here, I have been printing; and so long as I remain here, I shall keep on printing. In all probability, I shall die with a proof-sheet in my hand."

"This," said Flemming, closing the book, "is no caricature by a writer of comedy, but a portrait by a man's own hand. We can see by it how easily, under certain circumstances, one may glide into habits of seclusion, and in a kind of undress, slipshod hardihood, with a pipe and a proof-sheet, defy the world. Into this state scholars have too often fallen; thus giving some ground for the prevalent opinion, that scholarship and rusticity are inseparable. To me, I confess, it is painful to see the scholar and the world assume so often a hostile attitude, and set each other at defiance. Surely, it is a characteristic trait of a great and liberal mind, that it recognises humanity in all its forms and conditions. I am a student;—and always, when I sit alone at night, I recognise the divinity of the student, as she reveals herself to me in the smoke of the midnight lamp. But, because solitude and books are not unpleasant to me,—nay, wished-for,—sought after,—shall I say to my brother, Thou fool! Shall I take the world by the beard and say, Thou art old, and mad!—Shall I look society in the face and say, Thou art heartless!—Heartless! Beware of that word! Life, says very wisely the good Jean Paul, Life in every shape, should be precious to us, for the same reason that the Turks carefully collect every scrap of paper that comes in their way, because the name of God may be written upon it. Nothing is more true than this, yet nothing more neglected!"

"If it be painful to see this misunderstanding between scholars and the world," said the Baron, "I think it is still more painful to see the private sufferings of authors by profession. How many have languished in poverty, how many died broken-hearted, how many gone mad with over-excitement and disappointed hopes! How instructive and painfully interesting are their lives! with so many weaknesses,—so much to pardon,—so much to pity,—so much to admire! I think he was not so far out of the way, who said, that, next to the Newgate Calendar, the Biography of Authors is the most sickening chapter in the history of man."

"It is indeed enough to make one's heart ache!" interrupted Flemming. "Only think of Johnson and Savage, rambling about the streets of London at midnight, without a place to sleep in; Otway starved to death; Cowley mad, and howling like a dog, through the aisles of Chichester Cathedral, at the sound of church music; and Goldsmith, strutting up Fleet Street in his peach-blossom coat, to knock a bookseller over the pate with one of his own volumes; and then, in his poverty, about to marry his landlady in Green Arbour Court."

"A life of sorrow and privation, a hard life, indeed, do these poor devil authors have of it," replied the Baron; "and then at last must get them to the work-house, or creep away into some hospital to die."

"After all," said Flemming with a sigh, "poverty is not a vice."

"But something worse," interrupted the Baron; "as Dufresny said, when he married his laundress, because he could not pay her bill. He was the author, as you know, of the opera of Lot; at whose representation the great pun was made;—I say the great pun, as we say the great ton of Heidelberg. As one of the performers was singing the line, `L'amour a vaincu Loth,' (vingt culottes,) a voice from the pit cried out, `Qu'il en donne une à l'auteur!'"

Flemming laughed at the unseasonable jest; and then, after a short pause, continued;

"And yet, if you look closely at the causes of these calamities of authors, you will find, that many of them spring from false and exaggerated ideas of poetry and the poetic character; and from disdain of common sense, upon which all character, worth having, is founded. This comes from keeping aloof from the world, apart from our fellow-men; disdainful of society, as frivolous. By too much sitting still the body becomes unhealthy; and soon the mind. This is nature's law. She will never see her children wronged. If the mind, which rules the body, ever forgets itself so far as to trample upon its slave, the slave is never generous enough to forgive the injury; but will rise and smite its oppressor. Thus has many a monarch mind been dethroned."

"After all," said the Baron, "we must pardon much to men of genius. A delicate organization renders them keenly susceptible to pain and pleasure. And then they idealize every thing; and, in the moonlight of fancy, even the deformity of vice seems beautiful."

"And this you think should be forgiven?"

"At all events it is forgiven. The world loves a spice of wickedness. Talk as you will about principle, impulse is more attractive, even when it goes too far. The passions of youth, like unhooded hawks, fly high, with musical bells upon their jesses; and we forget the cruelty of the sport in the dauntless bearing of the gallant bird."

"And thus doth the world and society corrupt the scholar!" exclaimed Flemming.

Here the Baron rang, and ordered a bottle of Prince Metternich. He then very slowly filled his pipe, and began to smoke. Flemming was lost in a day-dream.

CHAPTER VIII

Time has a Doomsday-Book, upon whose pages he is continually recording illustrious names. But, as often as a new name is written there, an old one disappears. Only a few stand in illuminated characters, never to be effaced. These are the high nobility of Nature,—Lords of the Public Domain of Thought. Posterity shall never question their titles. But those, whose fame lives only in the indiscreet opinion of unwise men, must soon be as well forgotten, as if they had never been. To this great oblivion must most men come. It is better, therefore, that they should soon make up their minds to this; well knowing, that, as their bodies must ere long be resolved into dust again, and their graves tell no tales of them; so must their names likewise be utterly forgotten, and their most cherished thoughts, purposes, and opinions have no longer an individual being among men; but be resolved and incorporated into the universe of thought. If, then, the imagination can trace the noble dust of heroes, till we find it stopping a beer-barrel, and know that

"Imperial Cæsar, dead and turned to clay,

May stop a hole to keep the wind away;"

not less can it trace the noble thoughts of great men, till it finds them mouldered into the common dust of conversation, and used to stop men's mouths, and patch up theories, to keep out the flaws of opinion. Such, for example, are all popular adages and wise proverbs, which are now resolved into the common mass of thought; their authors forgotten, and having no more an individual being among men.

It is better, therefore, that men should soon make up their minds to be forgotten, and look about them, or within them, for some higher motive, in what they do, than the approbation of men, which is Fame; namely, their duty; that they should be constantly and quietly at work, each in his sphere, regardless of effects, and leaving their fame to take care of itself. Difficult must this indeed be, in our imperfection; impossible perhaps to achieve it wholly. Yet the resolute, the indomitable will of man can achieve much,—at times even this victory over himself; being persuaded, that fame comes only when deserved, and then is as inevitable as destiny, for it is destiny.

It has become a common saying, that men of genius are always in advance of their age; which is true. There is something equally true, yet not so common; namely, that, of these men of genius, the best and bravest are in advance not only of their own age, but of every age. As the German prose-poet says, every possible future is behind them. We cannot suppose, that a period of time will ever come, when the world, or any considerable portion of it shall have come up abreast with these great minds, so as fully to comprehend them.

And oh! how majestically they walk in history; some like the sun, with all his travelling glories round him; others wrapped in gloom, yet glorious as a night with stars. Through the else silent darkness of the past, the spirit hears their slow and solemn footsteps. Onward they pass, like those hoary elders seen in the sublime vision of an earthly Paradise, attendant angels bearing golden lights before them, and, above and behind, the whole air painted with seven listed colors, as from the trail of pencils!

And yet, on earth, these men were not happy,—not all happy, in the outward circumstance of their lives. They were in want, and in pain, and familiar with prison-bars, and the damp, weeping walls of dungeons! Oh, I have looked with wonder upon those, who, in sorrow and privation, and bodily

discomfort, and sickness, which is the shadow of death, have worked right on to the accomplishment of their great purposes; toiling much, enduring much, fulfilling much;—and then, with shattered nerves, and sinews all unstrung, have laid themselves down in the grave, and slept the sleep of death,—and the world talks of them, while they sleep!

It would seem, indeed, as if all their sufferings had but sanctified them! As if the death-angel, in passing, had touched them with the hem of his garment, and made them holy! As if the hand of disease had been stretched out over them only to make the sign of the cross upon their souls! And as in the sun's eclipse we can behold the great stars shining in the heavens, so in this life eclipse have these men beheld the lights of the great eternity, burning solemnly and forever!

This was Flemming's reverie. It was broken by the voice of the Baron, suddenly exclaiming;

"An angel is flying over the house!—Here; in this goblet, fragrant as the honey of Hymettus, fragrant as the wild flowers in the Angel's Meadow, I drink to the divinity of thy dreams."

"This is all sunshine," said Flemming, as he drank. "The wine of the Prince, and the Prince of wines. By the way, did you ever read that brilliant Italian dithyrambic, Redi's Bacchus in Tuscany? an ode which seems to have been poured out of the author's soul, as from a golden pitcher,

`Filled with the wine
Of the vine
Benign,
That flames so red in Sansavine.'
He calls the Montepulciano the king of all wines."

"Prince Metternich," said the Baron, "is greater than any king in Italy; and I wonder, that this precious wine has never inspired a German poet to write a Bacchus on the Rhine. Many little songs we have on this theme, but none very extraordinary. The best are Max Schenkendorf's Song of the Rhine, and the Song of Rhine Wine, by Claudius, a poet who never drank Rhenish without sugar. We will drink for him a blessing on the Rhine."

And again the crystal lips of the goblets kissed each other, with a musical chime, as of evening bells at vintage-time from the villages on the Rhine. Of a truth, I do not much wonder, that the German poet Schiller loved to write by candle-light with a bottle of Rhine-wine upon the table. Nor do I wonder at the worthy schoolmaster Roger Ascham, when he says, in one of his letters from Germany to Mr. John Raven, of John's College; `Tell Mr. Maden I will drink with him now a carouse of wine; and would to God he had a vessel of Rhenish wine; and perchance, when I come to Cambridge, I will so provide here, that every year I will have a little piece of Rhenish wine.' Nor, in fine, do I wonder at the German Emperor of whom he speaks in another letter to the same John Raven, and says, `The Emperor drank the best that I ever saw; he had his head in the glass five times as long as any of us, and never drank less than a good quart at once of Rhenish wine.' These were scholars and gentlemen.

"But to resume our old theme of scholars and their whereabout," said the Baron, with an unusual glow, caught no doubt from the golden sunshine, imprisoned, like the student Anselmus, in the glass bottle; "where should the scholar live? In solitude or in society? In the green stillness of the country, where he can hear the heart of nature beat, or in the dark, gray city, where he can hear and feel the throbbing heart of man? I will make answer for him, and say, in the dark, gray city. Oh, they do greatly err, who

think, that the stars are all the poetry which cities have; and therefore that the poet's only dwelling should be in sylvan solitudes, under the green roof of trees. Beautiful, no doubt, are all the forms of Nature, when transfigured by the miraculous power of poetry; hamlets and harvest-fields, and nut-brown waters, flowing ever under the forest, vast and shadowy, with all the sights and sounds of rural life. But after all, what are these but the decorations and painted scenery in the great theatre of human life? What are they but the coarse materials of the poet's song? Glorious indeed is the world of God around us, but more glorious the world of God within us. There lies the Land of Song; there lies the poet's native land. The river of life, that flows through streets tumultuous, bearing along so many gallant hearts, so many wrecks of humanity;—the many homes and households, each a little world in itself, revolving round its fireside, as a central sun; all forms of human joy and suffering, brought into that narrow compass;—and to be in this and be a part of this; acting, thinking, rejoicing, sorrowing, with his fellow-men;—such, such should be the poet's life. If he would describe the world, he should live in the world. The mind of the scholar, also, if you would have it large and liberal, should come in contact with other minds. It is better that his armour should be somewhat bruised even by rude encounters, than hang forever rusting on the wall. Nor will his themes be few or trivial, because apparently shut in between the walls of houses, and having merely the decorations of street scenery. A ruined character is as picturesque as a ruined castle. There are dark abysses and yawning gulfs in the human heart, which can be rendered passable only by bridging them over with iron nerves and sinews, as Challey bridged the Savine in Switzerland, and Telford the sea between Anglesea and England, with chain bridges. These are the great themes of human thought; not green grass, and flowers, and moonshine. Besides, the mere external forms of Nature we make our own, and carry with us into the city, by the power of memory."

"I fear, however," interrupted Flemming, "that in cities the soul of man grows proud. He needs at times to be sent forth, like the Assyrian monarch, into green fields, `a wonderous wretch and weedless,' to eat green herbs, and be wakened and chastised by the rain-shower and winter's bitter weather. Moreover, in cities there is danger of the soul's becoming wed to pleasure, and forgetful of its high vocation. There have been souls dedicated to heaven from childhood and guarded by good angels as sweet seclusions for holy thoughts, and prayers, and all good purposes; wherein pious wishes dwelt like nuns, and every image was a saint; and yet in life's vicissitudes, by the treachery of occasion, by the thronging passions of great cities, have become soiled and sinful. They resemble those convents on the river Rhine, which have been changed to taverns; from whose chambers the pious inmates have long departed, and in whose cloisters the footsteps of travellers have effaced the images of buried saints, and whose walls are written over with ribaldry and the names of strangers, and resound no more with holy hymns, but with revelry and loud voices."

"Both town and country have their dangers," said the Baron; "and therefore, wherever the scholar lives, he must never forget his high vocation. Other artists give themselves up wholly to the study of their art. It becomes with them almost religion. For the most part, and in their youth, at least, they dwell in lands, where the whole atmosphere of the soul is beauty; laden with it as the air may be with vapor, till their very nature is saturated with the genius of their art. Such, for example, is the artist's life in Italy."

"I agree with you," exclaimed Flemming; "and such should be the Poet's everywhere; for he has his Rome, his Florence, his whole glowing Italy within the four walls of his library. He has in his books the ruins of an antique world,—and the glories of a modern one,—his Apollo and Transfiguration. He must neither forget nor undervalue his vocation; but thank God that he is a poet; and everywhere be true to himself, and to `the vision and the faculty divine' he feels within him."

"But, at any rate, a city life is most eventful," continued the Baron. "The men who make, or take, the lives of poets and scholars, always complain that these lives are barren of incidents. Hardly a literary biography begins without some such apology, unwisely made. I confess, however, that it is not made without some show of truth; if, by incidents, we mean only those startling events, which suddenly turn aside the stream of Time, and change the world's history in an hour. There is certainly a uniformity, pleasing or unpleasing, in literary life, which for the most part makes to-day seem twin-born with yesterday. But if, by incidents, you mean events in the history of the human mind, (and why not?) noiseless events, that do not scar the forehead of the world as battles do, yet change it not the less, then surely the lives of literary men are most eventful. The complaint and the apology are both foolish. I do not see why a successful book is not as great an event as a successful campaign; only different in kind, and not easily compared."

"Indeed," interrupted Flemming, "in no sense is the complaint strictly true, though at times apparently so. Events enough there are, were they all set down. A life, that is worth writing at all, is worth writing minutely. Besides, all literary men have not lived in silence and solitude;—not all in stillness, not all in shadow. For many have lived in troubled times, in the rude and adverse fortunes of the state and age, and could say with Wallenstein,

`Our life was but a battle and a march;
And, like the wind's blast, never-resting, homeless,
We stormed across the war convulsed earth.'

Of such examples history has recorded many; Dante, Cervantes, Byron, and others; men of iron; men who have dared to breast the strong breath of public opinion, and, like spectre-ships, come sailing right against the wind. Others have been puffed out by the first adverse wind that blew; disgraced and sorrowful, because they could not please others. Truly `the tears live in an onion, that should water such a sorrow.' Had they been men, they would have made these disappointments their best friends, and learned from them the needful lesson of self-reliance."

"To confess the truth," added the Baron, "the lives of literary men, with their hopes and disappointments, and quarrels and calamities, present a melancholy picture of man's strength and weakness. On that very account the scholar can make them profitable for encouragement,—consolation,—warning."

"And after all," continued Flemming, "perhaps the greatest lesson, which the lives of literary men teach us, is told in a single word; Wait!—Every man must patiently bide his time. He must wait. More particularly in lands, like my native land, where the pulse of life beats with such feverish and impatient throbs, is the lesson needful. Our national character wants the dignity of repose. We seem to live in the midst of a battle,—there is such a din,—such a hurrying to and fro. In the streets of a crowded city it is difficult to walk slowly. You feel the rushing of the crowd, and rush with it onward. In the press of our life it is difficult to be calm. In this stress of wind and tide, all professions seem to drag their anchors, and are swept out into the main. The voices of the Present say, Come! But the voices of the Past say, Wait! With calm and solemn footsteps the rising tide bears against the rushing torrent up stream, and pushes back the hurrying waters. With no less calm and solemn footsteps, nor less certainly, does a great mind bear up against public opinion, and push back its hurrying stream. Therefore should every man wait;—should bide his time. Not in listless idleness,—not in useless pastime,—not in querulous dejection; but in constant, steady, cheerful endeavours, always willing and fulfilling, and accomplishing his task, that, when the occasion comes, he may be equal to the occasion. And if it never comes, what

matters it? What matters it to the world whether I, or you, or another man did such a deed, or wrote such a book, so be it the deed and book were well done! It is the part of an indiscreet and troublesome ambition, to care too much about fame,—about what the world says of us. To be always looking into the faces of others for approval;—to be always anxious for the effect of what we do and say; to be always shouting to hear the echo of our own voices! If you look about you, you will see men, who are wearing life away in feverish anxiety of fame, and the last we shall ever hear of them will be the funeral bell, that tolls them to their early graves! Unhappy men, and unsuccessful! because their purpose is, not to accomplish well their task, but to clutch the `trick and fantasy of fame'; and they go to their graves with purposes unaccomplished and wishes unfulfilled. Better for them, and for the world in their example, had they known how to wait! Believe me, the talent of success is nothing more than doing what you can do well; and doing well whatever you do,—without a thought of fame. If it come at all, it will come because it is deserved, not because it is sought after. And, moreover, there will be no misgivings,—no disappointment,—no hasty, feverish, exhausting excitement."

Thus endeth the First Book of Hyperion. I make no record of the winter. Paul Flemming buried himself in books; in old, dusty books. He studied diligently the ancient poetic lore of Germany, from Frankish Legends of Saint George, and Saxon Rhyme-Chronicles, down through Nibelungen Lieds, and Helden-Buchs, and Songs of the Minnesingers and Mastersingers, and Ships of Fools, and Reinecke Foxes, and Death-Dances and Lamentations of Damned Souls, into the bright, sunny land of harvests, where, amid the golden grain and the blue corn-flowers, walk the modern bards, and sing.

BOOK II

Epigraph

"Something the heart must have to cherish,
Must love, and joy, and sorrow learn;
Something with passion clasp, or perish,
And in itself to ashes burn."

CHAPTER I

SPRING

It was a sweet carol, which the Rhodian children sang of old in Spring, bearing in their hands, from door to door, a swallow, as herald of the season;

"The Swallow is come!
The Swallow is come!
O fair are the seasons, and light
Are the days that she brings,
With her dusky wings,
And her bosom snowy white."

A pretty carol, too, is that, which the Hungarian boys, on the islands of the Danube, sing to the returning stork in Spring;

"Stork! Stork! poor Stork!
Why is thy foot so bloody?
A Turkish boy hath torn it;
Hungarian boy will heal it,
With fiddle, fife, and drum."

But what child has a heart to sing in this capricious clime of ours, where Spring comes sailing in from the sea, with wet and heavy cloud-sails, and the misty pennon of the East-wind nailed to the mast! Yet even here, and in the stormy month of March even, there are bright, warm mornings, when we open our windows to inhale the balmy air. The pigeons fly to and fro, and we hear the whirring sound of wings. Old flies crawl out of the cracks, to sun themselves; and think it is summer. They die in their conceit; and so do our hearts within us, when the cold sea-breath comes from the eastern sea; and again,

"The driving hail
Upon the window beats with icy flail."

The red-flowering maple is first in blossom, its beautiful purple flowers unfolding a fortnight before the leaves. The moose-wood follows, with rose-colored buds and leaves; and the dog-wood, robed in the white of its own pure blossoms. Then comes the sudden rain-storm; and the birds fly to and fro, and shriek. Where do they hide themselves in such storms? at what firesides dry their feathery cloaks? At the fireside of the great, hospitable sun, to-morrow, not before;—they must sit in wet garments until then.

In all climates Spring is beautiful. In the South it is intoxicating, and sets a poet beside himself. The birds begin to sing;—they utter a few rapturous notes, and then wait for an answer in the silent woods. Those green-coated musicians, the frogs, make holiday in the neighbouring marshes. They, too, belong to the orchestra of Nature; whose vast theatre is again opened, though the doors have been so long bolted with icicles, and the scenery hung with snow and frost, like cobwebs. This is the prelude, which announces the rising of the broad green curtain. Already the grass shoots forth. The waters leap with thrilling pulse through the veins of the earth; the sap through the veins of the plants and trees; and the blood through the veins of man. What a thrill of delight in spring-time! What a joy in being and moving! Men are at work in gardens; and in the air there is an odor of the fresh earth. The leaf-buds begin to swell and blush. The white blossoms of the cherry hang upon the boughs like snow-flakes; and ere long our next-door neighbours will be completely hidden from us by the dense green foliage. The May-flowers open their soft blue eyes. Children are let loose in the fields and gardens. They hold butter-cups under each others' chins, to see if they love butter. And the little girls adorn themselves with chains and curls of dandelions; pull out the yellow leaves to see if the schoolboy loves them, and blow the down from the leafless stalk, to find out if their mothers want them at home.

And at night so cloudless and so still! Not a voice of living thing,—not a whisper of leaf or waving bough,—not a breath of wind,—not a sound upon the earth nor in the air! And overhead bends the blue sky, dewy and soft, and radiant with innumerable stars, like the inverted bell of some blue flower, sprinkled with golden dust, and breathing fragrance. Or if the heavens are overcast, it is no wild storm of

wind and rain; but clouds that melt and fall in showers. One does not wish to sleep; but lies awake to hear the pleasant sound of the dropping rain.

It was thus the Spring began in Heidelberg.

A COLLOQUY

"And what think you of Tiedge's Urania," said the Baron smiling, as Paul Flemming closed the book, and laid it upon the table.

"I think," said Flemming, "that it is very much like Jean Paul's grandfather,—in the highest degree poor and pious."

"Bravo!" exclaimed the Baron. "That is the best criticism I have heard upon the book. For my part, I dislike the thing as much as Goethe did. It was once very popular, and lay about in every parlour and bed-room. This annoyed the old gentleman exceedingly; and I do not wonder at it. He complains, that at one time nothing was sung or said but this Urania. He believed in Immortality; but wished to cherish his belief in quietness. He once told a friend of his, that he had, however, learned one thing from all this talk about Tiedge and his Urania; which was, that the saints, as well as the nobility, constitute an aristocracy. He said he found stupid women, who were proud because they believed in Immortality with Tiedge, and had to submit himself to not a few mysterious catechizings and tea-table lectures on this point; and that he cut them short by saying, that he had no objection whatever to enter into another state of existence hereafter, but prayed only that he might be spared the honor of meeting any of those there, who had believed in it here; for, if he did, the saints would flock around him on all sides, exclaiming, Were we not in the right? Did we not tell you so? Has it not all turned out just as we said? And, with such a conceited clatter in his ears, he thought that, before the end of six months, he might die of ennui in Heaven itself."

"How shocked the good old ladies must have been," said Flemming.

"No doubt, their nerves suffered a little; but the young ladies loved him all the better for being witty and wicked; and thought if they could only marry him, how they would reform him."

"Bettina Brentano, for instance."

"O no! That happened long afterwards. Goethe was then a silver-haired old man of sixty. She had never seen him, and knew him only by his writings; a romantic girl of seventeen."

"And yet much in love with the Sexagenarian. And surely a more wild, fantastic, and, excuse me, German passion never sprang up in woman's breast. She was a flower, that worshipped the sun."

"She afterwards married Achim von Arnim, and is now a widow. And not the least singular part of the affair, is, that, having grown older, and I hope colder, she should herself publish the letters which passed between her and Goethe."

"Particularly the letter in which she describes her first visit to Weimar, and her interview with the hitherto invisible divinity of her dreams. The old gentleman took her upon his knees, and she fell asleep with her head upon his shoulder. It reminds me of Titania and Nick Bottom, begging your pardon, always, for comparing your All-sided-One to Nick Bottom. Oberon must have touched her eyes with the juice of Love-in-idleness. However, this book of Goethe's Correspondence with a Child is a very singular and valuable revelation of the feelings, which he excited in female hearts. You say she afterwards married Achim von Arnim?"

"Yes; and he and her brother, Clemens Brentano, published that wondrous book, the Boy's Wonder-Horn."

"The Boy's Wonder-Horn!" said Flemming, after a short pause, for the name seemed to have thrown him into a reverie;—"I know the book almost by heart. Of all your German books it is the one which produces upon my imagination the most wild and magic influence. I have a passion for ballads!"

"And who has not?" said the Baron with a smile. "They are the gypsy-children of song, born under green hedgerows, in the leafy lanes and by-paths of literature,—in the genial summer-time."

"Why do you say summer-time and not summer?" inquired Flemming. "The expression reminds me of your old Minnesingers;—of Heinrich von Ofterdingen, and Walter von der Vogelweide, and Count Kraft von Toggenburg, and your own ancestor, I dare say, Burkhart von Hohenfels. They were always singing of the gentle summer-time. They seem to have lived poetry, as well as sung it; like the birds who make their marriage beds in the voluptuous trees."

"Is that from Shakspere?"

"No; from Lope de Vega."

"You are deeply read in the lore of antiquity, and the Aubades and Watch-Songs of the old Minnesingers. What do you think of the shoe-maker poets that came after them,—with their guilds and singing-schools? It makes me laugh to think how the great German Helicon, shrunk to a rivulet, goes bubbling and gurgling over the pebbly names of Zwinger, Wurgendrussel, Buchenlin, Hellfire, Old Stoll, Young Stoll, Strong Bopp, Dang Brotscheim, Batt Spiegel, Peter Pfort, and Martin Gumpel. And then the Corporation of the Twelve Wise Masters, with their stumpfereime and klingende-reime, and their Hans Tindeisen's rosemary-weise; and Joseph Schmierer's flowery-paradise-weise, and Frauenlob's yellow-weise, and blue-weise, and frog-weise, and looking-glass-weise!"

"O, I entreat you," exclaimed Flemming, laughing, "do not call those men poets! You transport me to quaint old Nuremberg, and I see Hans Sachs making shoes, and Hans Folz shaving the burgomaster."

"By the way," interrupted the Baron, "did you ever read Hoffmann's beautiful story of Master Martin, the Cooper of Nuremberg? I will read it to you this very night. It is the most delightful picture of that age, which you can conceive. But look! the sun has already set behind the Alsatian hills. Let us go up to the castle and look for the ghost in Prince Ruprecht's tower. O, what a glorious sunset!"

Flemming looked at the evening sky, and a shade of sadness stole over his countenance. He told not to his friend the sorrow, with which his heart was heavy; but kept it for himself alone. He knew that the

time, which comes to all men,—the time to suffer and be silent,—had come to him likewise; and he spake no word. O well has it been said, that there is no grief like the grief which does not speak.

CHAPTER III

OWL-TOWERS

"There sits the old Frau Himmelhahn, perched up in her owl-tower," said the Baron to Flemming, as they passed along the Hauptstrasse. "She looks down through her round-eyed spectacles from her nest up there, and watches every one that goes by. I wonder what mischief she is hatching now? Do you know she has nearly ruined your character in town? She says you have a rakish look, because you carry a cane, and your hair curls. Your gloves, also, are a shade too light for a strictly virtuous man."

"It is very kind in her to take such good care of my character, particularly as I am a stranger in town. She is doubtless learned in the Clothes-Philosophy."

"And ignorant of every thing else. She asked a friend of mine the other day, whether Christ was a Catholic or a Protestant."

"That is really too absurd!"

"Not too absurd to be true. And, ignorant as she is, she contrives to do a good deal of mischief in the course of the year. Why, the ladies already call you Wilhelm Meister."

"They are at liberty to call me what they please. But you, who know me better, know that I am something more than they would imply by the name."

"She says, moreover, that the American ladies sit with their feet out of the window, and have no pocket-handkerchiefs."

"Excellent!"

They crossed the market-place and went up beneath the grand terrace into the court-yard of the castle.

"Let us go up and sit under the great linden-trees, that grow on the summit of the Rent Tower," said Flemming. "From that point as from a watch-tower we can look down into the garden, and see the crowd below us."

"And amuse ourselves, as old Frau Himmelhahn does, at her window in the Hauptstrasse," added the Baron.

The keeper's daughter unlocked for them the door of the tower, and, climbing the steep stair-case, they seated themselves on a wooden bench under the linden-trees.

"How beautifully these trees overgrow the old tower! And see what a solid mass of masonry lies in the great fosse down there, toppled from its base by the explosion of a mine! It is like a rusty helmet cleft in twain, but still crested with towering plumes!"

"And what a motley crowd in the garden! Philisters and Sons of the Muses! And there goes the venerable Thibaut, taking his evening stroll. Do you see him there, with his silver hair flowing over his shoulders, and that friendly face, which has for so many years pored over the Pandects. I assure you, he inspires me with awe. And yet he is a merry old man, and loves his joke, particularly at the expense of Moses and other ancient lawgivers."

Here their attention was diverted by a wild-looking person, who passed with long strides under the archway in the fosse, right beneath them, and disappeared among the bushes. He was ill-dressed,—his hair flying in the wind,—his movements hurried and nervous, and the expression of his broad countenance wild, strange, and earnest.

"Who can that be!" asked Flemming. "He strides away indignantly, like one of Ossian's ghosts?"

"A great philosopher, whose name I have forgotten. Truly a strange owl!"

"He looks like a lion with a hat on."

"He is a mystic, who reads Schubert's History of the Soul, and lives, for the most part, in the clouds of the Middle Ages. To him the spirit-world is still open. He believes in the transmigration of souls; and I dare say is now following the spirit of some departed friend, who has taken the form of yonder pigeon."

"What a strange hallucination! He lives, I suppose, in the land of cloud-shadows. And, as St. Thomas Aquinas was said to be lifted up from the ground by the fervor of his prayers, so, no doubt, is he by the fervor of his visions."

"He certainly appears to neglect all sublunary things; and, to judge from certain appearances, since you seem fond of holy similitudes, one would say, that, like St. Serapion the Sindonite, he had but one shirt. Yet what cares he? he lives in that poetic dream-land of his thoughts, and clothes his dream-children in poetry."

"He is a poet, then, as well as a philosopher?"

"Yes; but a poet who never writes a line. There is nothing in nature to which his imagination does not give a poetic hue. But the power to make others see these objects in the same poetic light, is wanting. Still he is a man of fine powers and feelings; for, next to being a great poet, is the power of understanding one,—of finding one's-self in him, as we Germans say."

Three figures, dressed in black, now came from one of the green alleys, and stopped on the brink of a little fountain, that was playing among the gay flowers in the garden. The eldest of the three was a lady in that season of life, when the early autumn gives to the summer leaves a warmer glow, yet fades them not. Though the mother of many children, she was still beautiful;—resembling those trees, which blossom in October, when the leaves are changing, and whose fruit and blossom are on the branch at once. At her side was a girl of some sixteen years, who seemed to lean upon her arm for support. Her figure was slight; her countenance beautiful, though deadly white; and her meek eyes like the flower of

the night-shade, pale and blue, but sending forth golden rays. They were attended by a tall youth of foreign aspect, who seemed a young Antinous, with a mustache and a nose à la Kosciusko. In other respects a perfect hero of romance.

"Unless mine eyes deceive me," said the Baron, "there is the Frau von Ilmenau, with her pale daughter Emma, and that eternal Polish Count. He is always hovering about them, playing the unhappy exile, merely to excite that poor girl's sympathies; and as wretched as genius and wantonness can make him."

"Why, he is already married, you know," replied Flemming. "And his wife is young and beautiful."

"That does not prevent him from being in love with some one else. That question was decided in the Courts of Love in the Middle Ages. Accordingly he has sent his fair wife to Warsaw. But how pale the poor child looks."

"She has just recovered from severe illness. In the winter, you know, it was thought she would not live from hour to hour."

"And she has hardly recovered from that disease, before she seems threatened with a worse one; namely, a hopeless passion. However, people do not die of love now-a-days."

"Seldom, perhaps," said Flemming. "And yet it is folly to pretend that one ever wholly recovers from a disappointed passion. Such wounds always leave a scar. There are faces I can never look upon without emotion. There are names I can never hear spoken without almost starting!"

"But whom have we here?"

"That is the French poet Quinet, with his sweet German wife; one of the most interesting women I ever knew. He is the author of a very wild Mystery, or dramatic prose-poem, in which the Ocean, Mont-Blanc, and the Cathedral of Strassburg have parts to play; and the saints on the stained windows of the minster speak, and the statues and dead kings enact the Dance of Death. It is entitled Ahasuerus, or the Wandering Jew."

"Or, as the Danes would translate it, the Shoemaker of Jerusalem. That would be a still more fantastic title for his fantastic book. You know I am no great admirer of the modern French school of writers. The tales of Paul de Kock, who is, I believe, the most popular of all, seem to me like obscene stories told at dinner-tables, after the ladies have retired. It has been well said of him, that he is not only populaire but populacier; and equally well said of George Sand and Victor Hugo, that their works stand like fortifications, well built and well supplied with warlike munitions; but ineffectual against the Grand Army of God, which marches onward, as if nothing had happened. In surveying a national literature, the point you must start from, is national character. That lets you into many a secret; as, for example, Paul de Kock's popularity. The most prominent trait in the French character, is love of amusement, and excitement; and—"

"I should say, rather, the fear of ennui," interrupted Flemming. "One of their own writers has said with a great deal of truth, that the gentry of France rush into Paris to escape from ennui, as, in the noble days of chivalry, the defenceless inhabitants of the champaign fled into the castles, at the approach of some plundering knight, or lawless Baron; forsaking the inspired twilight of their native groves, for the luxurious shades of the royal gardens. What do you think of that?"

The Baron replied with a smile;

"There is only one Paris; and out of Paris there is no salvation for decent people."

Thus conversing of many things, sat the two friends under the linden-trees on the Rent Tower, till gradually the crowd disappeared from the garden, and the objects around them grew indistinct, in the fading twilight. Between them and the amber-colored western sky, the dense foliage of the trees looked heavy and hard, as if cast in bronze; and already the evening stars hung like silver lamps in the towering branches of that Tree of Life, brought more than two centuries ago from its primeval Paradise in America, to beautify the gardens of the Palatinate.

"I take a mournful pleasure in gazing at that tree," said Flemming, as they rose to depart. "It stands there so straight and tall, with iron bands around its noble trunk and limbs, in silent majesty, or whispering only in its native tongue, and freighting the homeward wind with sighs! It reminds me of some captive monarch of a savage tribe, brought over the vast ocean for a show, and chained in the public market-place of the city, disdainfully silent, or breathing only in melancholy accents a prayer for his native forest, a longing to be free."

"Magnificent!" cried the Baron. "I always experience something of the same feeling when I walk through a conservatory. The luxuriant plants of the tropics,—those illustrious exotics, with their gorgeous, flamingo-colored blossoms, and great, flapping leaves, like elephant's ears,—have a singular working upon my imagination; and remind me of a menagerie and wild-beasts kept in cages. But your illustration is finer;—indeed, a grand figure. Put it down for an epic poem."

CHAPTER IV

A BEER-SCANDAL

On their way homeward, Flemming and the Baron passed through a narrow lane, in which was a well-known Studenten-Kneipe. At the door stood a young man, whom the Baron at once recognised as his friend Von Kleist. He was a student; and universally acknowledged, among his young acquaintance, as a "devilish handsome fellow"; notwithstanding a tremendous scar on his cheek, and a cream-colored mustache, as soft as the silk of Indian corn. In short he was a renowner, and a duellist.

"What are you doing here, Von Kleist?"

"Ah, my dear Baron! Is it you? Come in; come in. You shall see some sport. A Fox-Commerce is on foot, and a regular Beer-Scandal."

"Shall we go in, Flemming?"

"Certainly. I should like to see how these things are managed in Heidelberg. You are a Baron, and I am a stranger. It is of no consequence what you and I do, as the king's fool Angeli said to the poet Bautru, urging him to put on his hat at the royal dinner-table."

William Lilly, the Astrologer, says, in his Autobiography, that, when he was committed to the guard-room in White Hall, he thought himself in hell; for "some were sleeping, others swearing, others smoking tobacco; and in the chimney of the room there were two bushels of broken tobacco-pipes, and almost half a load of ashes." What he would have thought if he had peeped into this Heidelberg Studenten-Kneipe, I know not. He certainly would not have thought himself in heaven; unless it were a Scandinavian heaven. The windows were open; and yet so dense was the atmosphere with the smoke of tobacco, and the fumes of beer, that the tallow candles burnt but dimly. A crowd of students were sitting at three long tables, in the large hall; a medley of fellows, known at German Universities under the cant names of Old-Ones, Mossy-Heads, Princes of Twilight, and Pomatum-Stallions. They were smoking, drinking, singing, screaming, and discussing the great Laws of the Broad-Stone and the Gutter. They had a great deal to say, likewise, about Besens, and Zobels, and Poussades; and, if they had been charged for the noise they made, as travellers used to be, in the old Dutch taverns, they would have had a longer bill to pay for that, than for their beer.

In a large arm-chair, upon the middle table, sat one of those distinguished individuals, known among German students as a Senior, or Leader of a Landsmannschaft. He was booted and spurred, and wore a very small crimson cap, and a very tight blue jacket, and very long hair, and a very dirty shirt. He was President of the night; and, as Flemming entered the hall with the Baron and his friend, striking upon the table with a mighty broadsword, he cried in a loud voice;

"Silentium!"

At the same moment a door at the end of the hall was thrown open, and a procession of newcomers, or Nasty-Foxes, as they are called in the college dialect, entered two by two, looking wild, and green, and foolish. As they came forward, they were obliged to pass under a pair of naked swords, held cross-wise by two Old-Ones, who, with pieces of burnt cork, made an enormous pair of mustaches, on the smooth, rosy cheeks of each, as he passed beneath this arch of triumph. While the procession was entering the hall, the President lifted up his voice again, and began to sing the well-known Fox-song, in the chorus of which all present joined lustily.

What comes there from the hill?
What comes there from the hill?
What comes there from the leathery hill?
Ha! Ha!
Leathery hill!
What comes there from the hill?
It is a postilion!
It is a postilion!
It is a leathery postilion!
Ha! Ha!
Postilion!
It is a postilion!
What brings the postilion?
What brings the postilion?
What brings the leathery postilion?
Ha! Ha!
Postilion!
What brings the postilion?

He bringeth us a Fox!
He bringeth us a Fox!
He bringeth us a leathery Fox!
Ha! Ha!
Leathery Fox!
He bringeth us a Fox!
Your servant, Masters mine!
Your servant, Masters mine!
Your servant, much-honored Masters mine!
Ha! Ha!
Much-honored Masters mine!
Your servant, Masters mine!
How does the Herr Papa?
How does the Herr Papa?
How does the leathery Herr Papa?
Ha! Ha!
Herr Papa!
How does the Herr Papa?
He reads in Cicero!
He reads in Cicero!
He reads in leathery Cicero!
Ha! Ha!
Cicero!
He reads in Cicero!
How does the Frau Mama?
How does the Frau Mama?
How does the leathery Frau Mama?
Ha! Ha!
Frau Mama!
How does the Frau Mama?
She makes the Papa tea!
She makes the Papa tea!
She makes the Papa leathery tea!
Ha! Ha!
Leathery tea!
She makes the Papa tea!
How does the Mamsell Sœur?
How does the Mamsell Sœur?
How does the leathery Mamsell Sœur?
Ha! Ha!
Mamsell Sœur!
How does the Mamsell Sœur?
She knits the Papa stockings!
She knits the Papa stockings!
She knits the Papa leathery stockings!
Ha! Ha!
Leathery stockings!
She knits the Papa stockings!

How does the Herr Rector?
How does the Herr Rector?
How does the leathery Herr Rector?
Ha! Ha!
Herr Rector!
How does the Herr Rector?
He calls the scholar, Boy!
He calls the scholar, Boy!
He calls the scholar, leathery Boy!
Ha! Ha!
Leathery Boy!
He calls the scholar, Boy!
And smokes the Fox tobacco?
And smokes the Fox tobacco?
And smokes the leathery Fox tobacco?
Ha! Ha!
Fox tobacco!
And smokes the Fox tobacco?
A little, Masters mine!
A little, Masters mine!
A little, much-honored Masters mine!
Ha! Ha!
Much-honored Masters mine!
A little, Masters mine!
Then let him fill a pipe!
Then let him fill a pipe!
Then let him fill a leathery pipe!
Ha! Ha!
Leathery pipe!
Then let him fill a pipe!
O Lord! It makes me sick!
O Lord! It makes him sick!
O Lord! It makes me leathery sick!
Ha! Ha!
Leathery sick!
O Lord! It makes me sick!
Then let him throw it off!
Then let him throw it off!
Then let him throw it leathery off!
Ha! Ha!
Leathery off!
Then let him throw it off!
Now I again am well!
Now he again is well!
Now I again am leathery well!
Ha! Ha!
Leathery well!
Now I again am well!

So grows the Fox a Bursch!
So grows the Fox a Bursch!
So grows the leathery Fox a Bursch!
Ha! Ha!
Fox a Bursch!
So grows the Fox a Bursch!

At length the song was finished. Meanwhile large tufts and strips of paper had been twisted into the hair of the Branders, as those are called who have been already one semestre at the University, and then at a given signal were set on fire, and the Branders rode round the table on sticks, amid roars of laughter. When this ceremony was completed, the President rose from his chair, and in a solemn voice pronounced a long discourse, in which old college jokes were mingled with much parental advice to young men on entering life, and the whole was profusely garnished with select passages from the Old Testament. Then they all seated themselves at the table and the heavy beer-drinking set in, as among the Gods and Heroes of the old Northern mythology.

"Brander! Brander!" screamed a youth, whose face was hot and flushed with supper and with beer; "Brander, I say? Thou art a Doctor! No,—a Pope;—thou art a Pope, by—"

These words were addressed to a pale, quiet-looking person, who sat opposite, and was busy in making a wretched, shaved poodle sit on his hind legs in a chair, by his master's side, and hold a short clay pipe in his mouth,—a performance to which the poodle seemed no wise inclined.

"Thou art challenged!" replied the pale Student, turning from his dog, who dropped the pipe from his mouth and leaped under the table.

Seconds were chosen on the spot; and the arms ordered; namely, six mighty goblets, or Bassgläser, filled to the brim with foaming beer. Three were placed before each duellist.

"Take your weapons!" cried one of the seconds, and each of the combatants seized a goblet in his hand.

"Strike!"

And the glasses rang, with a salutation like the crossing of swords.

"Set to!"

Each set the goblet to his lips.

"Out!"

And each poured the contents down his throat, as if he were pouring them through a tunnel into a beer-barrel. The other two glasses followed in quick succession, hardly a long breath drawn between. The pale Student was victorious. He was first to drain the third goblet. He held it for a moment inverted, to let the last drops fall out, and then placing it quietly on the table, looked his antagonist in the face, and said;

"Hit!"

Then, with the greatest coolness, he looked under the table and whistled for his dog. His antagonist stopped midway in his third glass. Every vein in his forehead seemed bursting; his eyes were wild and bloodshot, his hand gradually loosened its hold upon the table, and he sank and rolled together like a sheet of lead. He was drunk.

At this moment a majestic figure came stalking down the table, ghost-like, through the dim, smoky atmosphere. His coat was off, his neck bare, his hair wild, his eyes wide open, and looking right before him, as if he saw some beckoning hand in the air, that others could not see. His left hand was upon his hip, and in his right he held a drawn sword extended, and pointing downward. Regardless of every one, erect, and with a martial stride he marched directly along the centre of the table, crushing glasses and overthrowing bottles at every step. The students shrunk back at his approach; till at length one more drunk, or more courageous, than the rest, dashed a glass full of beer into his face. A general tumult ensued, and the student with the sword leaped to the floor. It was Von Kleist. He was renowning it. In the midst of the uproar could be distinguished the offensive words;

"Arrogant! Absurd! Impertinent! Dummer Junge!"

Von Kleist went home that night with no less than six duels on his hands. He fought them all out in as many days; and came off with only a gash through his upper lip and another through his right eyelid from a dexterous Suabian Schlaeger.

CHAPTER V

THE WHITE LADY'S SLIPPER AND THE PASSION-FLOWER

That night Emma of Ilmenau went to her chamber with a heavy heart, and her dusky eyes were troubled with tears. She was one of those gentle beings, who seem created only to love and to be loved. A shade of melancholy softened her character. She shunned the glare of daylight and of society, and wished to be alone. Like the evening primrose, her heart opened only after sunset; but bloomed through the dark night with sweet fragrance. Her mother, on the contrary, flaunted in the garish light of society. There was no sympathy between them. Their souls never approached, never understood each other, and words were often spoken which wounded deeply. And therefore Emma of Ilmenau went to her chamber that night with tears in her eyes.

She was followed by her French chamber-maid, Madeleine, a native of Strassburg, who had grown old in the family. In her youth, she had been poor,—and virtuous because she had never been tempted; and, now that she had grown old, and seen no immediate reward for her virtue, as is usual with weak minds, she despaired of Providence, and regretted she had never been tempted. Whilst this unfortunate personage was lighting the wax tapers on the toilet, and drawing the bed-curtains, and tattling about the room, Emma threw herself into an arm-chair, and, crossing her hands in her lap, and letting her head fall upon her bosom, seemed lost in a dream.

"Why have these gentle feelings been given me!" said she in her heart. "Why have I been born with all these warm affections,—these ardent longings after what is good, if they lead only to sorrow and disappointment? I would love some one;—love him once and forever;—devote myself to him alone,—

live for him,—die for him,— exist alone in him! But alas! in all this wide world there is none to love me, as I would be loved,—none whom I may love, as I am capable of loving. How empty, how desolate, seems the world about me! Why has Heaven given me these affections, only to fall and fade!"

Alas! poor child! thou too must learn like others, that the sublime mystery of Providence goes on in silence, and gives no explanation of itself,—no answer to our impatient questionings!

"Bless me, child, what ails you?" exclaimed Madeleine, perceiving that Emma paid no attention to her idle gossip. "When I was of your age—"

"Do not talk to me now, good Madeleine. Leave me, I wish to be alone?"

"Well, here is something," continued the maid, taking a billet from her bosom, "which I hope will enliven you. When I was of your age—"

"Hush! hush!" said Emma, taking the billet from the hard hand of Madeleine. "Once more I beg you, leave me! I wish to be alone!"

Madeleine took the lamp and retired slowly, wishing her young mistress many good nights and rosy dreams. Emma broke the seal of the note. As she read, her face became deadly pale, and then, as quick as thought, a crimson blush gleamed on her cheek, and her hands trembled. Tenderness, pity, love, offended pride, the weakness and dignity of woman, were all mingled in her look, changing and passing over her fine countenance like cloud-shadows. She sunk back in her chair, covering her face with her hands, as if she would hide it from herself and Heaven.

"He loves me!" said she to herself; "loves me; and is married to another, whom he loves not! and dares to tell me this! O, never,— never,—never! And yet he is so friendless and alone in this unsympathizing world,—and an exile, and homeless! I can but pity him;—yet I hate him, and will see him no more!"

This short reverie of love and hate was broken by the sound of a clear, mellow voice, which, in the universal stillness of the hour, seemed almost like the voice of a spirit. It was a voice, without the accompaniment of any instrument, singing those sweet lines of Goethe;

"Under the tree-tops is quiet now!
In all the woodlands hearest thou
Not a sound!
The little birds are asleep in the trees,
Wait! wait! and soon like these,
Sleepest thou!"

Emma knew the voice and started. She rushed to the window to close it. It was a beautiful night, and the stars were shining peacefully over the mountain of All-Saints. The sound of the Neckar was soft and low, and nightingales were singing among the brown shadows of the woods. The large red moon shone, like a ruby, in the horizon's ample ring; and golden threads of light seemed braided together with the rippling current of the river. Tall and spectral stood the white statues on the bridge. The outline of the hills, the castle, the arches of the bridge, and the spires and roofs of the town were as strongly marked as if cut out of pasteboard. Amid this fairy scene, a little boat was floating silently down the stream. Emma closed the window hastily, and drew the curtains close.

"I hate him; and yet I will pray for him," said she, as she laid her weary head upon that pillow, from which, but a few months before, she thought she should never raise it again. "O, that I had died then! I dare not love him, but I will pray for him!"

Sweet child! If the face of the deceiver comes so often between thee and Heaven, I tremble for thy fate! The plant that sprang from Helen's tears destroyed serpents;—would that from thine might spring up heart's-ease;—some plant, at least, to destroy the serpents in thy bosom. Believe me, upon the margin of celestial streams alone, those simples grow, which cure the heartache!

And this the silent stars beheld, looking down from heaven, and told it not again. This, likewise, the Frau Himmelhahn beheld, looking from her chamber-window, and was not so discreet as the silent stars.

CHAPTER VI

GLIMPSES INTO CLOUD-LAND

"There are many things, which, having no corporeal evidence, can be perceived and comprehended only by the discursive energies of reason. Hence the ambiguous nature of matter can be comprehended only by adulterated opinion. Matter is the principle of all bodies, and is stamped with the impression of forms. Fire, air, and water derive their origin and principle from the scalene triangle. But the earth was created from right-angled triangles, of which two of the sides are equal. The sphere and the pyramid contain in themselves the figure of fire; but the octaedron was destined to be the figure of air, and the icosaedron of water. The right-angled isosceles triangle produces from itself a square, and the square generates from itself the cube, which is the figure peculiar to earth. But the figure of a beautiful and perfect sphere was imparted to the most beautiful and perfect world, that it might be indigent of nothing, but contain all things, embracing and comprehending them in itself, and thus might be excellent and admirable, similar to and in concord with itself, ever moving musically and melodiously. If I use a novel language, excuse me. As Apuleius says, pardon must be granted to novelty of words, when it serves to illustrate the obscurity of things."

These words came from the lips of the lion-like philosopher, who has been noticed before in these pages. He was sitting with Flemming, smoking a long pipe. As the Baron said, he was indeed a strange owl; for the owl is a grave bird; a monk, who chants midnight mass in the great temple of Nature;—an anchorite,—a pillar saint,—the very Simeon Stylites of his neighbourhood. Such, likewise, was the philosophical Professor. Solitary, but with a mighty current, flowed the river of his life, like the Nile, without a tributary stream, and making fertile only a single strip in the vast desert. His temperament had been in youth a joyous one; and now, amid all his sorrows and privations, for he had many, he looked upon the world as a glad, bright, glorious world. On the many joys of life he gazed still with the eyes of childhood, from the far-gone Past upward, trusting, hoping;—and upon its sorrows with the eyes of age, from the distant Future, downward, triumphant, not despairing. He loved solitude, and silence, and candle-light, and the deep midnight. "For," said he, "if the morning hours are the wings of the day, I only fold them about me to sleep more sweetly; knowing that, at its other extremity, the day, like the fowls of the air, has an epicurean morsel,—a parson's nose; and on this oily midnight my spirit revels and is glad."

Such was the Professor, who had been talking in a half-intelligible strain for two hours or more. The Baron had fallen fast asleep in his chair; but Flemming sat listening with excited imagination, and the Professor continued in the following words, which, to the best of his listener's memory, seemed gleaned here and there from Fichte's Destiny of Man, and Shubert's History of the Soul.

"Life is one, and universal; its forms many and individual. Throughout this beautiful and wonderful creation there is never-ceasing motion, without rest by night or day, ever weaving to and fro. Swifter than a weaver's shuttle it flies from Birth to Death, from Death to Birth; from the beginning seeks the end, and finds it not, for the seeming end is only a dim beginning of a new out-going and endeavour after the end. As the ice upon the mountain, when the warm breath of the summer sun breathes upon it, melts, and divides into drops, each of which reflects an image of the sun; so life, in the smile of God's love, divides itself into separate forms, each bearing in it and reflecting an image of God's love. Of all these forms the highest and most perfect in its god-likeness is the human soul. The vast cathedral of Nature is full of holy scriptures, and shapes of deep, mysterious meaning; but all is solitary and silent there; no bending knee, no uplifted eye, no lip adoring, praying. Into this vast cathedral comes the human soul, seeking its Creator; and the universal silence is changed to sound, and the sound is harmonious, and has a meaning, and is comprehended and felt. It was an ancient saying of the Persians, that the waters rush from the mountains and hurry forth into all the lands to find the Lord of the Earth; and the flame of the Fire, when it awakes, gazes no more upon the ground, but mounts heavenward to seek the Lord of Heaven; and here and there the Earth has built the great watch-towers of the mountains, and they lift their heads far up into the sky, and gaze ever upward and around, to see if the Judge of the World comes not! Thus in Nature herself, without man, there lies a waiting, and hoping, a looking and yearning, after an unknown somewhat. Yes; when, above there, where the mountain lifts its head over all others, that it may be alone with the clouds and storms of heaven, the lonely eagle looks forth into the gray dawn, to see if the day comes not! when, by the mountain torrent, the brooding raven listens to hear if the chamois is returning from his nightly pasture in the valley; and when the soon uprising sun calls out the spicy odors of the thousand flowers, the Alpine flowers, with heaven's deep blue and the blush of sunset on their leaves;—then there awakes in Nature, and the soul of man can see and comprehend it, an expectation and a longing for a future revelation of God's majesty. It awakens, also, when in the fulness of life, field and forest rest at noon, and through the stillness is heard only the song of the grasshopper and the hum of the bee; and when at evening the singing lark, up from the sweet-smelling vineyards rises, or in the later hours of night Orion puts on his shining armour, to walk forth in the fields of heaven. But in the soul of man alone is this longing changed to certainty and fulfilled. For lo! The light of the sun and the stars shines through the air, and is nowhere visible and seen; the planets hasten with more than the speed of the storm through infinite space, and their footsteps are not heard, but where the sunlight strikes the firm surface of the planets, where the storm wind smites the wall of the mountain cliff, there is the one seen and the other heard. Thus is the glory of God made visible, and may be seen, where in the soul of man it meets its likeness changeless and firm-standing. Thus, then, stands Man;—a mountain on the boundary between two worlds;—its foot in one, its summit far-rising into the other. From this summit the manifold landscape of life is visible, the way of the Past and Perishable, which we have left behind us; and, as we evermore ascend, bright glimpses of the daybreak of Eternity beyond us!"

Flemming would fain have interrupted this discourse at times, to answer and inquire, but the Professor went on, warming and glowing more and more. At length, there was a short pause, and Flemming said;

"All these indefinite longings,—these yearnings after an unknown somewhat, I have felt and still feel within me; but not yet their fulfilment."

"That is because you have not faith;" answered the Professor. "The Present is an age of doubt and disbelief, and darkness; out of which shall arise a clear and bright Hereafter. In the second part of Goethe's Faust, there is a grand and striking scene, where in the classical Walpurgis Night, on the Pharsalian Plains, the mocking Mephistopheles sits down between the solemn antique Sphinxes, and boldly questions them, and reads their riddles. The red light of innumerable watch-fires glares all round about, and shines upon the terrible face of the arch-scoffer; while on either side, severe, majestic, solemnly serene, we behold the gigantic forms of the children of Chimæra, half buried in the earth, their mild eyes gazing fixedly, as if they heard through the midnight, the swift-rushing wings of the Stymphalides, striving to outstrip the speed of Alcides' arrows! Angry griffins are near them; and not far are Sirens, singing their wondrous songs from the rocking branches of the willow trees! Even thus does a scoffing and unbelieving Present sit down, between an unknown Future and a too believing Past, and question and challenge the gigantic forms of faith, half buried in the sands of Time, and gazing forward steadfastly into the night, whilst sounds of anger and voices of delight alternate vex and soothe the ear of man!—But the time will come, when the soul of man shall return again childlike and trustful to its faith in God; and look God in the face and die; for it is an old saying, full of deep, mysterious meaning, that he must die, who hath looked upon a God. And this is the fate of the soul, that it should die continually. No sooner here on earth does it awake to its peculiar being, than it struggles to behold and comprehend the Spirit of Life. In the first dim twilight of its existence, it beholds this spirit, is pervaded by its energies,—is quick and creative like the spirit itself, and yet slumbers away into death after having seen it. But the image it has seen, remains, in the eternal procreation, as a homogeneal existence, is again renewed, and the seeming death, from moment to moment, becomes the source of kind after kind of existences in ever-ascending series. The soul aspires ever onward to love and to behold. It sees the image more perfect in the brightening twilight of the dawn, in the ever higher-rising sun. It sleeps again, dying in the clearer vision; but the image seen remains as a permanent kind; and the slumberer awakes anew and ever higher after its own image, till at length, in the full blaze of noonday, a being comes forth, which, like the eagle, can behold the sun and die not. Then both live on, even when this bodily element, the mist and vapor through which the young eagle gazed, dissolves and falls to earth."

"I am not sure that I understand you," said Flemming; "but if I do, you mean to say, that, as the body continually changes and takes unto itself new properties, and is not the same to-day as yesterday, so likewise the soul lays aside its idiosyncrasies, and is changed by acquiring new powers, and thus may be said to die. And hence, properly speaking, the soul lives always in the Present, and has, and can have, no Future; for the Future becomes the Present, and the soul that then lives in me is a higher and more perfect soul; and so onward forevermore."

"I mean what I say," continued the Professor; "and can find no more appropriate language to express my meaning than that which I have used. But as I said before, pardon must be granted to the novelty of words, when it serves to illustrate the obscurity of things. And I think you will see clearly from what I have said, that this earthly life, when seen hereafter from heaven, will seem like an hour passed long ago, and dimly remembered;—that long, laborious, full of joys and sorrows as it is, it will then have dwindled down to a mere point, hardly visible to the far-reaching ken of the disembodied spirit. But the spirit itself soars onward. And thus death is neither an end nor a beginning. It is a transition not from one existence to another, but from one state of existence to another. No link is broken in the chain of being; any more than in passing from infancy to manhood, from manhood to old age. There are seasons of reverie and deep abstraction, which seem to me analogous to death. The soul gradually loses its consciousness of what is passing around it; and takes no longer cognizance of objects which are near. It seems for the moment to have dissolved its connexion with the body. It has passed as it were into

another state of being. It lives in another world. It has flown over lands and seas; and holds communion with those it loves, in distant regions of the earth, and the more distant heaven. It sees familiar faces, and hears beloved voices, which to the bodily senses are no longer visible and audible. And this likewise is death; save that when we die, the soul returns no more to the dwelling it has left."

"You seem to take it for granted," interrupted Flemming, "that, in our reveries, the soul really goes out of the body into distant places, instead of summoning up their semblance within itself by the power of memory and imagination!"

"Something I must take for granted," replied the Professor. "We will not discuss that point now. I speak not without forethought. Just observe what a glorious thing human life is, when seen in this light; and how glorious man's destiny. I am; thou art; he is! seems but a school-boy's conjugation. But therein lies a great mystery. These words are significant of much. We behold all round about us one vast union, in which no man can labor for himself without laboring at the same time for all others; a glimpse of truth, which by the universal harmony of things becomes an inward benediction, and lifts the soul mightily upward. Still more so, when a man regards himself as a necessary member of this union. The feeling of our dignity and our power grows strong, when we say to ourselves; My being is not objectless and in vain; I am a necessary link in the great chain, which, from the full development of consciousness in the first man, reaches forward into eternity. All the great, and wise, and good among mankind, all the benefactors of the human race, whose names I read in the world's history, and the still greater number of those, whose good deeds have outlived their names,—all those have labored for me. I have entered into their harvest. I walk the green earth, which they inhabited. I tread in their footsteps, from which blessings grow. I can undertake the sublime task, which they once undertook, the task of making our common brotherhood wiser and happier. I can build forward, where they were forced to leave off; and bring nearer to perfection the great edifice which they left uncompleted. And at length I, too, must leave it, and go hence. O, this is the sublimest thought of all! I can never finish the noble task; therefore, so sure as this task is my destiny, I can never cease to work, and consequently never cease to be. What men call death cannot break off this task, which is never-ending; consequently no period is set to my being, and I am eternal. I lift my head boldly to the threatening mountain peaks, and to the roaring cataract, and to the storm-clouds swimming in the fire-sea overhead and say; I am eternal, and defy your power! Break, break over me! and thou Earth, and thou Heaven, mingle in the wild tumult! and ye Elements foam and rage, and destroy this atom of dust,—this body, which I call mine! My will alone, with its fixed purpose, shall hover brave and triumphant over the ruins of the universe; for I have comprehended my destiny; and it is more durable than ye! It is eternal; and I, who recognise it, I likewise am eternal! Tell me, my friend, have you no faith in this?"

"I have;" answered Flemming, and there was another pause. He then said;

"I have listened to you patiently and without interruption. Now listen to me. You complain of the skepticism of the age. This is one form in which the philosophic spirit of the age presents itself. Let me tell you, that another form, which it assumes, is that of poetic reverie. Plato of old had dreams like these; and the Mystics of the Middle Ages; and still their disciples walk in the cloud-land and dream-land of this poetic philosophy. Pleasant and cool upon their souls lie the shadows of the trees under which Plato taught. From their whispering leaves comes wafted across the noise of populous centuries a solemn and mysterious sound, which to them is the voice of the Soul of the World. All nature has become spiritualized and transfigured; and, wrapt in beautiful, vague dreams of the real and the ideal, they live in this green world, like the little child in the German tale, who sits by the margin of a woodland lake, and hears the blue heaven and the branches overhead dispute with their reflection in

the water, which is the reality and which the image. I willingly confess, that such day-dreams as these appeal strongly to my imagination. Visitants and attendants are they of those lofty souls, which, soaring ever higher and higher, build themselves nests under the very eaves of the stars, forgetful that they cannot live on air, but must descend to earth for food. Yet I recognise them as day-dreams only; as shadows, not substantial things. What I mainly dislike in the New Philosophy, is the cool impertinence with which an old idea, folded in a new garment, looks you in the face and pretends not to know you, though you have been familiar friends from childhood. I remember an English author who, in speaking of your German Philosophies, says very wisely; `Often a proposition of inscrutable and dread aspect, when resolutely grappled with, and torn from its shady den, and its bristling entrenchments of uncouth terminology,—and dragged forth into the open light of day, to be seen by the natural eye and tried by merely human understanding, proves to be a very harmless truth, familiar to us from old, sometimes so familiar as to be a truism. Too frequently the anxious novice is reminded of Dryden in the Battle of the Books; there is a helmet of rusty iron, dark, grim, gigantic; and within it, at the farthest corner, is a head no bigger than a walnut.'—Can you believe, that these words ever came from the lips of Carlyle! He has himself taken up the uncouth terminology of late; and many pure, simple minds are much offended at it. They seem to take it as a personal insult. They are angry; and deny the just meed of praise. It is, however, hardly worth while to lose our presence of mind. Let us rather profit as we may, even from this spectacle, and recognise the monarch in his masquerade. For, hooded and wrapped about with that strange and antique garb, there walks a kingly, a most royal soul, even as the Emperor Charles walked amid solemn cloisters under a monk's cowl;—a monarch still in soul. Such things are not new in the history of the world. Ever and anon they sweep over the earth, and blow themselves out soon, and then there is quiet for a season, and the atmosphere of Truth seems more serene. Why would you preach to the wind? Why reason with thunder-showers? Better sit quiet, and see them pass over like a pageant, cloudy, superb, and vast."

The Professor smiled self-complacently, but said not a word. Flemming continued;

"I will add no more than this;—there are many speculations in Literature, Philosophy, and Religion, which, though pleasant to walk in, and lying under the shadow of great names, yet lead to no important result. They resemble rather those roads in the western forests of my native land, which, though broad and pleasant at first, and lying beneath the shadow of great branches, finally dwindle to a squirrel track, and run up a tree!"

The Professor hardly knew whether he should laugh or be offended at this sally; and, laying his hand upon Flemming's arm, he said seriously;

"Believe me, my young friend, the time will come, when you will think more wisely on these things. And with you, I trust, that time will soon come; since it moves more speedily with some than with others. For what is Time? The shadow on the dial,—the striking of the clock,—the running of the sand,—day and night,—summer and winter,—months, years, centuries! These are but arbitrary and outward signs,—the measure of Time, not Time itself! Time is the Life of the Soul. If not this, then tell me what it is?"

The high and animated tone of voice in which the Professor uttered these words aroused the Baron from his sleep; and, not distinctly comprehending what was said, but thinking the Professor asked what time it was, he innocently exclaimed;

"I should think it must be near midnight!"

This somewhat disconcerted the Professor, who took his leave soon afterward. When he was gone the Baron said;

"Excuse me for treating your guest so cavalierly. His transcendentalism annoyed me not a little; and I took refuge in sleep. One would think, to judge by the language of this sect, that they alone saw any beauty in Nature; and, when I hear one of them discourse, I am instantly reminded of Goethe's Baccalaureus, when he exclaims; `The world was not before I created it; I brought the sun up out of the sea; with me began the changeful course of the moon; the day decked itself on my account; the earth grew green and blossomed to meet me; at my nod in that first night, the pomp of all the stars developed itself; who but I set you free from all the bonds of Philisterlike, contracting thoughts? I, however, emancipated as my mind assures me I am, gladly pursue my inward light, advance boldly in a transport peculiarly my own, the bright before me, and the dark behind!'—Do you not see a resemblance? O, they might be modest enough to confess, that one straggling ray of light may, by some accident, reach the blind eyes of even us poor, benighted heathens?"

"Alas! how little veneration we have!" said Flemming. "I could not help closing the discussion with a jest. An ill-timed levity often takes me by surprise. On all such occasions I think of a scene at the University, where, in the midst of a grave discussion on the possibility of Absolute Motion, a scholar said he had seen a rock split open, from which sprang a toad, who could not be supposed to have any knowledge of the external world, and consequently his motion must have been absolute. The learned Professor, who presided on that occasion, was hardly more startled and astonished, than was our learned Professor, five minutes ago. But come; wind up your watch, and let us go to bed."

"By the way," said the Baron, "did you mind what a curious head he has. There are two crowns upon it."

"That is a sign," replied Flemming, "that he will eat his bread in two kingdoms."

"I think the poor man would be very thankful," said the Baron with a smile, "if he were always sure of eating it in one. He is what the Transcendentalists call a god-intoxicated man; and I advise him, as Sauteul advised Bossuet, to go to Patmos and write a new Apocalypse."

CHAPTER VII

MILL-WHEELS AND OTHER WHEELS

A few days after this the Baron received letters from his sister, telling him, that her physicians had prescribed a few weeks at the Baths of Ems, and urging him to meet her there before the fashionable season.

"Come," said he to Flemming; "make this short journey with me. We will pass a few pleasant days at Ems, and visit the other watering-places of Nassau. It will drive away the melancholy day-dreams that haunt you. Perhaps some future bride is even now waiting for you, with dim presentiments and undefined longings, at the Serpent's Bath."

"Or some widow of Ems, with a cork-leg!" said Flemming, smiling; and then added, in a tone of voice half jest, half earnest, "Certainly; let us go in pursuit of her;—

'Whoe'er she be,
That not impossible she,
That shall command my heart and me.
Where'er she lie,
Hidden from mortal eye,
In shady leaves of destiny.'"

They started in the afternoon for Frankfort, pursuing their way slowly along the lovely Bergstrasse, famed throughout Germany for its beauty. They passed the ruined house where Martin Luther lay concealed after the Diet of Worms, and through the village of Handschuhsheimer, as old as the days of King Pepin the Short,—a hamlet, lying under the hills, half-buried in blossoms and green leaves. Close on the right rose the mountains of the mysterious Odenwald; and on the left lay the Neckar, like a steel bow in the meadow. Farther westward, a thin, smoky vapor betrayed the course of the Rhine; beyond which, like a troubled sea, ran the blue, billowy Alsatian hills. Song of birds, and sound of evening bells, and fragrance of sweet blossoms filled the air; and silent and slow sank the broad red sun, half-hidden amid folding clouds.

"We shall not pass the night at Weinheim," said the Baron to the postilion, who had dismounted to walk up the hill, leading to the town. "You may drive to the mill in the Valley of Birkenau."

The postilion seized one of his fat horses by the tail, and swung himself up to his seat again. They rattled through the paved streets of Weinheim, and took no heed of the host of the Golden Eagle, who stood so invitingly at the door of his own inn; and the ruins of Burg Windeck, above there, on its mountain throne, frowned at them for hurrying by, without staying to do him homage.

"The old ruin looks well from the valley," said the Baron; "but let us beware of climbing that steep hill. Most travellers are like children; they must needs touch whatever they behold. They climb up to every old broken tooth of a castle, which they find on their way;—get a toilsome ascent and hot sunshine for their pains, and come down wearied and disappointed. I trust we are wiser."

They crossed the bridge, and turned up the stream, passing under an arch of stone, which serves as a gateway to this enchanted Valley of Birkenau. A cool and lovely valley! shut in by high hills;—shaded by alder-trees and tall poplars, under which rushes the Wechsnitz, a noisy mountain brook, that ever and anon puts its broad shoulder to the wheel of a mill, and shows that it can labor as well as laugh. At one of these mills they stopped for the night.

A mill forms as characteristic a feature in the romantic German landscape, as in the romantic German tale. It is not only a mill, but likewise an ale-house and rural inn; so that the associations it suggests are not of labor only, but also of pleasure. It stands in the narrow defile, with its picturesque, thatched roof; thither throng the peasants, of a holiday; and there are rustic dances under the trees.

In the twilight of the fast-approaching summer night, the Baron and Flemming walked forth along the borders of the stream. As they heard it, rushing and gushing among the stones and tangled roots, and the great wheel turning in the current, with its never-ceasing plash! plash! it brought to their minds that exquisite, simple song of Goethe, the Youth and the Mill-brook. It was for the moment a nymph, which sang to them in the voice of the waters.

"I am persuaded," said Flemming, "that, in order fully to understand and fell the popular poetry of Germany, one must be familiar with the German landscape. Many sweet little poems are the outbreaks of momentary feelings;—words, to which the song of birds, the rustling of leaves, and the gurgle of cool waters form the appropriate music. Or perhaps I should say they are words, which man has composed to the music of nature. Can you not, even now, hear this brooklet telling you how it is on its way to the mill, where at day-break the miller's daughter opens her window, and comes down to bathe her face in its stream, and her bosom is so full and white, that it kindles the glow of love in the cool waters!"

"A most delightful ballad, truly," said the Baron. "But like many others of our little songs, it requires a poet to fell and understand it. Sing them in the valley and woodland shadows, and under the leafy roofs of garden walks, and at night, and alone, as they were written. Sing them not in the loud world,—for the loud world laughs such things to scorn. It is Mueller who says, in that little song, where the maiden bids the moon good evening;

`This song was made to be sung at night,
And he who reads it in broad daylight,
Will never read the mystery right;
And yet it is childlike easy!'

He has written a great many pretty songs, in which the momentary, indefinite longings and impulses of the soul of man find an expression. He calls them the songs of a Wandering Horn-player. There is one among them much to our present purpose. He expresses in it, the feeling of unrest and desire of motion, which the sight and sound of running waters often produce in us. It is entitled, `Whither?' and is worth repeating to you.

`I heard a brooklet gushing
From its rocky fountain near,
Down into the valley rushing,
So fresh and wondrous clear.

`I know not what came o'er me,
Nor who the counsel gave;
But I must hasten downward,
All with my pilgrim-stave.

`Downward, and ever farther,
And ever the brook beside;
And ever fresher murmured,
And ever clearer the tide.

`Is this the way I was going?
Whither, O brooklet, say!
Thou hast, with thy soft murmur,
Murmured my senses away.

`What do I say of a murmur?
That can no murmur be;
'T is the water-nymphs, that are singing

Their roundelays under me.

`Let them sing, my friend, let them murmur,
And wander merrily near;
The wheels of a mill are going
In every brooklet clear.'"

"There you have the poetic reverie," said Flemming, "and the dull prose commentary and explanation in matter of fact. The song is pretty; and was probably suggested by some such scene as this, which we are now beholding. Doubtless all your old national traditions sprang up in the popular mind as this song in the poet's."

"Your opinion is certainly correct," answered the Baron; "and yet all this play of poetic fancy does not prevent me from feeling the chill night air, and the pangs of hunger. Let us go back to the mill, and see what our landlady has for supper. Did you observe what a loud, sharp voice she has?"

"People always have, who live in mills, and near water-falls."

On the following morning they emerged unwillingly from the green, dark valley, and journeyed along the level highway to Frankfort, where in the evening they heard the glorious Don Giovanni of Mozart. Of all operas this was Flemming's favorite. What rapturous flights of sound! what thrilling, pathetic chimes! what wild, joyous revelry of passion! what a delirium of sense!—what an expression of agony and woe! all the feelings of suffering and rejoicing humanity sympathized with and finding a voice in those tones. Flemming and the Baron listened with ever-increasing delight.

"How wonderful this is!" exclaimed Flemming, transported by his feelings. "How the chorus swells and dies, like the wind of summer! How those passages of mysterious import seem to wave to and fro, like the swaying branches of trees; from which anon some solitary sweet voice darts off like a bird, and floats away and revels in the bright, warm sunshine! And then mark! how, amid the chorus of a hundred voices and a hundred instruments,—of flutes, and drums, and trumpets,—this universal shout and whirl-wind of the vexed air, you can so clearly distinguish the melancholy vibration of a single string, touched by the finger,—a mournful, sobbing sound! Ah, this is indeed human life! where in the rushing, noisy crowd, and amid sounds of gladness, and a thousand mingling emotions, distinctly audible to the ear of thought, are the pulsations of some melancholy string of the heart, touched by an invisible hand."

Then came, in the midst of these excited feelings, the ballet; drawing its magic net about the soul. And soon, from the tangled yet harmonious mazes of the dance, came forth a sylph-like form, her scarf floating behind her, as if she were fanning the air with gauze-like wings. Noiseless as a feather or a snow-flake falls, did her feet touch the earth. She seemed to float in the air, and the floor to bend and wave under her, as a branch, when a bird alights upon it, and takes wing again. Loud and rapturous applause followed each wonderful step, each voluptuous movement; and, with a flushed cheek and burning eye, and bosom panting to be free, stood the gracefully majestic figure for a moment still, and then the winged feet of the swift dancing-girls glanced round her, and she was lost again in the throng.

"How truly exquisite this is!" exclaimed the Baron, after joining loudly in the applause. "What a noble figure! What grace! what attitudes! How much soul in every motion! how much expression in every gesture! I assure you, it produces upon me the same effect as a beautiful poem. It is a poem. Every step is a word; and the whole together a poem!"

The Baron and Flemming were delighted with the scene; and at the same time exceedingly amused with the countenance of an old prude in the next box, who seemed to look upon the wholemagic show, with such feelings as Michal, Saul's daughter, experienced, when she looked from her window and saw King David dancing and leaping with his scanty garments.

"After all," said Flemming, "the old French priest was not so far out of the way, when he said, in his coarse dialect, that the dance is the Devil's procession; and paint and ornaments, the whetting of the devil's sword; and the ring that is made in dancing, the devil's grindstone, whereon he sharpens his sword; and finally, that a ballet is the pomp and mass of the Devil, and whosoever entereth therein, entereth into his pomp and mass; for the woman who singeth is the prioress of the Devil, and they that answer are clerks, and they that look on are parishioners, and the cymbals and flutes are the bells, and the musicians that play are the ministers, of the Devil."

"No doubt this good lady near us, thinks so likewise," answered the Baron laughing; "but she likes it, for all that."

When the play was over the Baron begged Flemming to sit still, till the crowd had gone.

"I have a strange fancy," said he, "whenever I come to the theatre, to see the end of all things. When the crowd is gone, and the curtain raised again to air the house, and the lamps are all out, save here and there one behind the scenes, the contrast with what has gone before is most impressive. Every thing wears a dream-like aspect. The empty boxes and stalls,—the silence,—the smoky twilight, and the magic scene dismantled, produce in me a strange, mysterious feeling. It is like a dim reflection of a theatre in water, or in a dusty mirror; and reminds me of some of Hoffmann's wild Tales. It is a practical moral lesson,—a commentary on the play, and makes the show complete."

It was truly as he said; only tenfold more desolate, solemn, and impressive; and produced upon the mind the effect we experience, when slumber is suddenly broken, and dreams and realities mingle, and we know not yet whether we sleep or wake. As they at length passed out through the dimly-lighted passage, they heard a vulgar-looking fellow, with a sensual face and shaggy whiskers, say to some persons who were standing near him, and seemed to be hangers-on of the play-house;

"I shall run her six nights at Munich, and then take her on to Vienna."

Flemming thought he was speaking of some favorite horse. He was speaking of his beautiful wife, the ballet-dancer.

CHAPTER VIII

OLD HUMBUG

What most interested our travellers in the ancient city of Frankfort, was neither the opera nor the Ariadne of Dannecker, but the house in which Goethe was born, and the scenes he frequented in his childhood, and remembered in his old age. Such for example are the walks around the city, outside the moat; the bridge over the Maine, with the golden cock on the cross, which the poet beheld and

marvelled at when a boy; the cloister of the Barefooted Friars, through which he stole with mysterious awe to sit by the oilcloth-covered table of old Rector Albrecht; and the garden in which his grandfather walked up and down among fruit-trees and rose-bushes, in long morning gown, black velvet cap, and the antique leather gloves, which he annually received as Mayor on Pipers-Doomsday, representing a kind of middle personage between Alcinous and Laertes. Thus, O Genius! are thy foot-prints hallowed; and the star shines forever over the place of thy nativity.

"Your English critics may rail as they list," said the Baron, while he and Flemming were returning from a stroll in the leafy gardens, outside the moat; "but, after all, Goethe was a magnificent old fellow. Only think of his life; his youth of passion, alternately aspiring and desponding, stormy, impetuous, headlong;—his romantic manhood, in which passion assumes the form of strength; assiduous, careful, toiling, without haste, without rest; and his sublime old age,—the age of serene and classic repose, where he stands like Atlas, as Claudian has painted him in the Battle of the Giants, holding the world aloft upon his head, the ocean-streams hard frozen in his hoary locks."

"A good illustration of what the world calls his indifferentism."

"And do you know I rather like this indifferentism? Did you never have the misfortune to live in a community, where a difficulty in the parish seemed to announce the end of the world? or to know one of the benefactors of the human race, in the very `storm and pressure period' of his indiscreet enthusiasm? If you have, I think you will see something beautiful in the calm and dignified attitude which the old philosopher assumes."

"It is a pity, that his admirers had not a little of this philosophic coolness. It amuses me to read the various epithets, which they apply to him; The Dear, dear Man! The Life-enjoying Man! The All-sided One! The Representative of Poetry upon earth! The Many-sided Master-Mind of Germany! His enemies rush into the other extreme, and hurl at him the fierce names of Old Humbug! and Old Heathen! which hit like pistol-bullets."

"I confess, he was no saint."

"No; his philosophy is the old ethnic philosophy. You will find it all in a convenient and concentrated, portable form in Horace's beautiful Ode to Thaliarcus. What I most object to in the old gentleman is his sensuality."

"O nonsense. Nothing can be purer than the Iphigenia; it is as cold and passionless as a marble statue."

"Very true; but you cannot say the same of some of the Roman Elegies and of that monstrous book the Elective Affinities."

"Ah, my friend, Goethe is an artist; and looks upon all things as objects of art merely. Why should he not be allowed to copy in words what painters and sculptors copy in colors and in marble?"

"The artist shows his character in the choice of his subject. Goethe never sculptured an Apollo, nor painted a Madonna. He gives us only sinful Magdalens and rampant Fauns. He does not so much idealize as realize."

"He only copies nature."

"So did the artists, who made the bronze lamps of Pompeii. Would you hang one of those in your hall? To say that a man is an artist and copies nature is not enough. There are two great schools of art; the imitative and the imaginative. The latter is the most noble, and most enduring; and Goethe belonged rather to the former. Have you read Menzel's attack upon him?"

"It is truly ferocious. The Suabian hews into him lustily. I hope you do not side with him."

"By no means. He goes too far. He blames the poet for not being a politician. He might as well blame him for not being a missionary to the Sandwich Islands."

"And what do you think of Eckermann?"

"I think he is a toady; a kind of German Boswell. Goethe knew he was drawing his portrait, and attitudinized accordingly. He works very hard to make a Saint Peter out of an old Jupiter, as the Catholics did at Rome."

"Well; call him Old Humbug, or Old Heathen, or what you please; I maintain, that, with all his errors and short-comings, he was a glorious specimen of a man."

"He certainly was. Did it ever occur to you that he was in some points like Ben Franklin? a kind of rhymed Ben Franklin? The practical tendency of his mind was the same; his love of science was the same; his benignant, philosophic spirit was the same; and a vast number of his little poetic maxims and sooth-sayings seem nothing more than the worldly wisdom of Poor Richard, versified."

"What most offends me is, that now every German jackass must have a kick at the dead lion."

"And every one who passes through Weimar must throw a book upon his grave, as travellers did of old a stone upon the grave of Manfredi, at Benevento. But, of all that has been said or sung, what most pleases me is Heine's Apologetic, if I may so call it; in which he says, that the minor poets, who flourished under the imperial reign of Goethe `resemble a young forest, where the trees first show their own magnitude after the oak of a hundred years, whose branches had towered above and overshadowed them, has fallen. There was not wanting an opposition, that strove against Goethe, this majestic tree. Men of the most warring opinions united themselves for the contest. The adherents of the old faith, the orthodox, were vexed, that, in the trunk of the vast tree, no niche with its holy image was to be found; nay, that even the naked Dryads of paganism were permitted to play their witchery there; and gladly, with consecrated axe, would they have imitated the holy Boniface, and levelled the enchanted oak to the ground. The followers of the new faith, the apostles of liberalism, were vexed on the other hand, that the tree could not serve as the Tree of Liberty, or, at any rate, as a barricade. In fact the tree was too high; no one could plant the red cap upon its summit, or dance the Carmagnole beneath its branches. The multitude, however, venerated this tree for the very reason, that it reared itself with such independent grandeur, and so graciously filled the world with its odor, while its branches, streaming magnificently toward heaven, made it appear, as if the stars were only the golden fruit of its wondrous limbs.' Don't you think that beautiful?"

"Yes, very beautiful. And I am glad to see, that you can find something to admire in my favorite author, notwithstanding his frailties; or, to use an old German saying, that you can drive the hens out of the garden without trampling down the beds."

"Here is the old gentleman himself!" exclaimed Flemming.

"Where!" cried the Baron, as if for the moment he expected to see the living figure of the poet walking before them.

"Here at the window,—that full-length cast. Excellent, is it not! He is dressed, as usual, in his long yellow nankeen surtout, with a white cravat crossed in front. What a magnificent head! and what a posture! He stands like a tower of strength. And, by Heavens! he was nearly eighty years old, when that was made."

"How do you know?"

"You can see by the date on the pedestal."

"You are right. And yet how erect he stands, with his square shoulders braced back, and his hands behind him. He looks as if he were standing before the fire. I feel tempted to put a live coal into his hand, it lies so invitingly half-open. Gleim's description of him, soon after he went to Weimar, is very different from this. Do you recollect it?"

"No, I do not."

"It is a story, which good old father Gleim used to tell with great delight. He was one evening reading the Göttingen Musen-Almanach in a select society at Weimar, when a young man came in, dressed in a short, green shooting-jacket, booted and spurred, and having a pair of brilliant, black, Italian eyes. He in turn offered to read; but finding probably the poetry of the Musen-Almanach of that year rather too insipid for him, he soon began to improvise the wildest and most fantastic poems imaginable, and in all possible forms and measures, all the while pretending to read from the book. `That is either Goethe or the Devil,' said good old father Gleim to Wieland, who sat near him. To which the `Great I of Osmannstadt' replied; `It is both, for he has the Devil in him to-night; and at such times he is like a wanton colt, that flings out before and behind, and you will do well not to go too near him!' "

"Very good!"

"And now that noble figure is but mould. Only a few months ago, those majestic eyes looked for the last time on the light of a pleasant spring morning. Calm, like a god, the old man sat; and with a smile seemed to bid farewell to the light of day, on which he had gazed for more than eighty years. Books were near him, and the pen which had just dropped, as it were from his dying fingers. `Open the shutters, and let in more light!' were the last words that came from those lips. Slowly stretching forth his hand, he seemed to write in the air; and, as it sank down again and was motionless, the spirit of the old man departed."

"And yet the world goes on. It is strange how soon, when a great man dies, his place is filled; and so completely, that he seems no longer wanted. But let us step in here. I wish to buy that cast; and send it home to a friend."

CHAPTER IX

After lingering a day or two in Frankfort, the two friends struck across through Hochheim to the Rhine, and then up among the hills of the Rheingau to Schlangenbad, where they tarried only to bathe, and to dine; and then pursued their way to Langenschwalbach. The town lies in a valley, with gently-sloping hills around it, and long avenues of poplars leading forth into the fields. One interminable street cuts the town in twain, and there are old houses with curious faces carved upon their fronts, and dates of the olden time.

Our travellers soon sallied forth from their hotel, impatient to drink the strength-giving waters of the fountains. They continued their walk far up the valley under the poplars. The new grain was waving in the fields; the birds singing in the trees and in the air; and every thing seemed glad, save a poor old man, who came tottering out of the woods, with a heavy bundle of sticks on his shoulders.

Returning upon their steps, they passed down the valley and through the long street to the tumble-down old Lutheran church. A flight of stone steps leads from the street to the green terrace or platform on which the church stands, and which, in ancient times, was the churchyard, or as the Germans more devoutly say, God's-acre; where generations are scattered like seeds, and that which is sown in corruption shall be raised hereafter in incorruption. On the steps stood an old man,—a very old man,— holding a little girl by the hand. He took off his greasy cap as they passed, and wished them good day. His teeth were gone; he could hardly articulate a syllable. The Baron asked him how old the church was. He gave no answer; but when the question was repeated, came close up to them, and taking off his cap again, turned his ear attentively, and said;

"I am hard of hearing."

"Poor old man," said Flemming; "He is as much a ruin as the church we are entering. It will not be long before he, too, shall be sown as seed in this God's-acre!"

The little girl ran into a house close at hand, and brought out the great key. The church door swung open, and, descending a few steps, they passed through a low-roofed passage into the church. All was in ruin. The gravestones in the pavement were started from their places; the vaults beneath yawned; the roof above was falling piecemeal; there were rents in the old tower; and mysterious passages, and side doors with crazy flights of wooden steps, leading down into the churchyard. Amid all this ruin, one thing only stood erect; it was a statue of a knight in armour, standing in a niche under the pulpit.

"Who is this?" said Flemming to the old sexton; "who is this, that stands here so solemnly in marble, and seems to be keeping guard over the dead men below?"

"I do not know," replied the old man; "but I have heard my grandfather say it was the statue of a great warrior!"

"There is history for you!" exclaimed the Baron. "There is fame! To have a statue of marble, and yet have your name forgotten by the sexton of your parish, who can remember only, that he once heard his grandfather say, that you were a great warrior!"

Flemming made no reply, for he was thinking of the days, when from that old pulpit, some bold reformer thundered down the first tidings of a new doctrine, and the roof echoed with the grand old hymns of Martin Luther.

When he communicated his thoughts to the Baron, the only answer he received was;

"After all, what is the use of so much preaching? Do you think the fishes, that heard the sermon of St. Anthony, were any better than those who did not? I commend to your favorable notice the fish-sermon of this saint, as recorded by Abraham à Santa Clara. You will find it in your favorite Wonder-Horn."

Thus passed the day at Langenschwalbach; and the evening at the Allée-Saal was quite solitary; for as yet no company had arrived to fill its chambers, or sit under the trees before the door. The next morning even Flemming and the Baron were gone; for the German's heart was beating with strong desire to embrace his sister; and the heart of his friend cared little whither he went, so be it he were not too much alone.

After a few hours' drive, they were looking down from the summit of a hill right upon the house-tops of Ems. There it lay, deep sunk in the hollow beneath them, as if some inhabitant of Sirius, like him spoken of in Voltaire's tale of Micromegas, held it in the hollow of his hand. High and peaked rise the hills, that throw their shadows into this romantic valley, and at their base winds the river Lahn. Our travellers drove through the one long street, composed entirely of hotels and lodging-houses. Sick people looked out of the windows, as they passed. Others were walking leisurely up and down, beneath the few decapitated trees, which represent a public promenade; and a boy, with a blue frock and crimson cap, was driving three donkeys down the street. In short, they were in a fashionable watering-place; as yet sprinkled only by a few pattering drops of the summer rain of strangers, which generally follows the first hot days.

On alighting at the London Hotel, the Baron found—not his sister, but only a letter from her, saying she had changed her mind and gone to the Baths of Franconia. This was a disappointment, which the Baron pocketed with the letter, and said not a word more about either. It was his way; his life-philosophy in small things and great. In the evening, they went to an æsthetic tea, at the house of the Frau Kranich, the wife of a rich banker of Frankfort.

"I must tell you about this Frau Kranich," said the Baron to Flemming, on the way. "She is a woman of talent and beauty, and just in the prime of life. But, unfortunately, very ambitious. Her mania is, to make a figure in the fashionable world; and to this end she married a rich banker of Frankfort, old enough to be her father, not to say her grandfather, hoping, doubtless, that he would soon die; for, if ever a woman wished to be a widow, she is that woman. But the old fellow is tough and won't die. Moreover, he is deaf, and crabbed, and penurious, and half the time bed-ridden. The wife is a model of virtue, notwithstanding her weakness. She nurses the old gentleman as if he were a child. And, to crown all, he hates society, and will not hear of his wife's receiving or going into company."

"How, then, can she give soirées?" asked Flemming.

"I was just going to tell you," continued the Baron. "The gay lady has no taste for long evenings with the old gentleman in the back chamber;—for being thus chained like a criminal under Mezentius, face to face with a dead body. So she puts him to bed first, and—"

"Gives him opium."

"Yes, I dare say; and then gives herself a soirée, without his knowing any thing about it. This course of deception is truly hateful in itself, and must be particularly so to her, for she is not a low, or an immoral woman; but one of those who, not having strength enough to complete the sacrifice they have had strength enough to commence, are betrayed into a life of duplicity and falsehood."

They had now reached the house, and were ushered into a room gaily lighted and filled with guests. The hostess came forward to receive them, dressed in white, and sailing down the room like a swan. When the customary salutations had passed and Flemming had been duly presented, the Baron said, not without a certain degree of malice;

"And, my dear Frau Kranich, how is your good husband to night?"

This question was about as discreet as a cannon-ball. But the lady replied in the simplicity of her heart, and not in the least disconcerted;

"The same as ever, my dear Baron. It is astonishing how he holds out. But let us not talk of these things now. I must introduce your friend to his countryman, the Grand Duke of Mississippi; alike remarkable for his wealth, his modesty, and the extreme simplicity of his manners. He drives only six horses. Besides, he is known as a man of learning and piety;—has his private chapel, and private clergyman, who always preaches against the vanity of worldly riches. He has also a private secretary, whose sole duty is to smoke to him, that he may enjoy the aroma of Spanish cigars, without the trouble of smoking."

"Decidedly a man of genius!"

Here Flemming was introduced to his illustrious countryman; a person who seemed to consist chiefly of linen, such a display did he make of collar, bosom, and wristbands.

"Pray, Mr. Flemming, what do you think of that Rembrandt?" said he, pointing to a picture on the wall. "Exquisite picture! The grandeur of sentiment and splendor of chiaroscuro are of the first order. Just observe the liquidity of the water, and the silveryness of the clouds! Great power! There is a bravura of handling in that picture, Sir, which requires the eye of the connoisseur to appreciate."

"Yes, a most undoubted—copy!"

And here their conversation ended; for at that moment the little Moldavian Prince Jerkin made his way through the crowd, with his snuff-box as usual in his hand, and hurried up to Flemming whom he had known in Heidelberg. He was eager to let every one know that he spoke English, and in his haste began by making a mistake.

"Good bye! Good bye! Mr. Flemming!" said he, instead of good evening. "I am ravished to see you in Ems. Nice place;—all that there is of most nice. I drink my water and am good! Do you not think the Frau Kranich has a very beautiful leather?"

He meant skin. Flemming laughed outright; but it was not perceived by the Prince, because at that moment he was pushed aside, in the rush of a gallopade, and Flemming beheld his face no more. At the same moment the Baron introduced a friend of his, who also spoke English and said;

"You will sup with me to-night. I have some Rhine-wine, which will be a seduction to you."

Soon after, the Baron stood with an impassioned, romantic lady leaning on his arm, examining a copy of Raphael's Fornarina.

"Ach! I wish I had been the Fornarina," sighed the impassioned, romantic lady.

"Then, my dear Madam," replied the Baron, "I wish I had been Raphael."

And so likewise said to himself a very tall man with fiery red hair, and fancy whiskers, who was waltzing round and round in one spot, and in a most extraordinary waistcoat; thus representing a fiery, floating-light, to warn men of the hidden rocks, on which the breath of vanity drives them shipwreck. At length, his partner, tired of spinning, sank upon a sofa, like a child's top, when it reels and falls.

"You do not like the waltz?" said an elderly French gentleman, remarking the expression of Flemming's countenance.

"O yes; among the figurantes of the Opera. But I confess, it sometimes makes me shudder to see a young rake clasp his arms round the waist of a pure and innocent girl. What would you say, were you to see him sitting on a sofa with his arms round your wife?"

"Mere prejudice of education," replied the French gentleman. "I know that situation. I have read all about it in the Bibliothèque de Romans Choisis!"

And merrily went the dance; and bright eyes and flushed cheeks were not wanting among the dancers;

"And they waxed red, and waxed warm,

And rested, panting, arm in arm,"

and the Strauss-walzes sounded pleasantly in the ears of Flemming, who, though he never danced, yet, like Henry of Ofterdingen, in the Romance of Novalis, thought to music. The wheeling waltz set the wheels of his fancy going. And thus the moments glided on, and the footsteps of Time were not heard amid the sound of music and voices.

But suddenly this scene of gayety was interrupted. The door opened wide; and the short figure of a gray-haired old man presented itself, with a flushed countenance and wild eyes. He was but half-dressed, and in his hand held a silver candlestick without a light. A sheet was wound round his head, like a turban; and he tottered forward with a vacant, bewildered look, exclaiming;

"I am Mahomet, the king of the Jews!"

At the same moment he fell in a swoon; and was borne out of the room by the servants. Flemming looked at the lady of the festival, and she was deadly pale. For a moment all was confusion; and the dance and the music stopped. The impression produced on the company was at once ludicrous and awful. They tried in vain to rally. The whole society was like a dead body, from which the spirit has

departed. Ere long the guests had all dispersed, and left the lady of the mansion to her mournful, expiring lamps, and still more mournful reflections.

"Truly," said Flemming, to the Baron, as they wended their way homeward, "this seems not like reality; but like one of the sharp contrasts we find in novels. Who shall say, after this, that there is not more romance in real life, than we find written in books!"

"Not more romance," said the Baron, "but a different romance."

A still more tragic scene had been that evening enacted in Heidelberg. Just as the sun set, two female figures walked along the romantic woodland path-way, leading to the Angel's Meadow, a little green opening on the brow of one of the high hills, which see themselves in the Neckar and hear the solemn bells of Kloster-Neuburg. The evening shadows were falling broad and long; and the cuckoo began to sing.

"Cuckoo! Cuckoo!" said the eldest of the two figures, repeating an old German popular rhyme,

`Cuckoo! Cuckoo!
Tell me true,
Tell me fair and fine,
How long must I unmarried pine!'"

It was the voice of an evil spirit, that spoke in the person of Madeleine; and the pale and shrinking figure, that walked by her side, and listened to those words, was Emma of Ilmenau. A young man joined them, where the path turns into the thick woodlands; and they disappeared among the shadowy branches. It was the Polish Count.

The forget-me-nots looked up to heaven with their meek blue eyes, from their home in the Angel's Meadow. Calmly stood the mountain of All-Saints, in its majestic, holy stillness;—the river flowed so far below, that the murmur of its waters was not heard;—there was not a sigh of the evening wind among the leaves,—not a sound upon the earth nor in the air;—and yet that night there fell a star from heaven!

CHAPTER X

THE PARTING

It was now that season of the year, which an old English writer calls the amiable month of June, and at that hour of the day, when, face to face, the rising moon beholds the setting sun. As yet the stars were few in heaven. But, after the heat of the day, the coolness and the twilight descended like a benediction upon the earth, by all those gentle sounds attended, which are the meek companions of the night.

Flemming and the Baron had passed the afternoon at the Castle. They had rambled once more together, and for the last time, over the magnificent ruin. On the morrow they were to part, perhaps forever. The Baron was going to Berlin, to join his sister; and Flemming, driven forward by the restless spirit within him, longed once more for a change of scene, and was going to the Tyrol and Switzerland. Alas! he never

said to the passing hour; "Stay, for thou art fair!" but reached forward into the dark future, with unsatisfied longings and aimless desires, that were never still.

As the day was closing, they sat down on the terrace of Elisabeth's Garden. The sun had set beyond the blue Alsatian hills; and on the valley of the Rhine fell the purple mist, like the mantle of the departing prophet from his fiery chariot. Over the castle walls, and the trees of the garden, rose the large moon; and between the contending daylight and moonlight there were as yet no shadows. But at length the shadows came; transparent and faint outlines, that deepened into form. In the valley below only the river gleamed, like steel; and here and there the lamps were lighted in the town. Solemnly stood the leafy linden trees in the garden near them, their trunks in darkness and their summits bronzed with moonlight; and in his niche in the great round tower, overhung with ivy, like a majestic phantom, stood the gray statue of Louis, with his venerable beard, and shirt of mail, and flowing mantle; and the mild, majestic countenance looked forth into the silent night, as the countenance of a seer, who reads the stars. At intervals the wind of the summer night passed through the ruined castle and the trees, and they sent forth a sound as if nature were sighing in her dreams; and for a moment overhead the broad leaves gently clashed together, like brazen cymbals, with a tinkling sound; and then all was still, save the sweet, passionate song of nightingales, that nowhere upon earth sing more sweetly than in the gardens of Heidelberg Castle.

The hour, the scene, and the near-approaching separation of the two young friends, had filled their hearts with a pleasant, though at the same time not painless excitement. They had been conversing about the magnificent old ruin, and the ages in which it had been built, and the vicissitudes of time and war, that had battered down its walls, and left it "tenantless, save to the crannying wind."

"How sorrowful and sublime is the face of that statue yonder," said Flemming. "It reminds me of the old Danish hero Beowulf; for careful, sorrowing, he seeth in his son's bower the wine-hall deserted, the resort of the wind, noiseless; the knight sleepeth; the warrior lieth in darkness; there is no noise of the harp, no joy in the dwellings, as there was before."

"Even as you say," replied the Baron; "but it often astonishes me, that, coming from that fresh green world of yours beyond the sea, you should feel so much interest in these old things; nay, at times, seem so to have drunk in their spirit, as really to live in the times of old. For my part, I do not see what charm there is in the pale and wrinkled countenance of the Past, so to entice the soul of a young man. It seems to me like falling in love with one's grandmother. Give me the Present;—warm, glowing, palpitating with life. She is my mistress; and the Future stands waiting like my wife that is to be, for whom, to tell the truth, I care very little just now. Indeed, my friend, I wish you would take more heed of this philosophy of mine; and not waste the golden hours of youth in vain regrets for the past, and indefinite, dim longings for the future. Youth comes but once in a lifetime."

"Therefore," said Flemming; "let us so enjoy it as to be still young when we are old. For my part, I grow happier as I grow older. When I compare my sensations and enjoyments now, with what they were ten years ago, the comparison is vastly in favor of the present. Much of the fever and fretfulness of life is over. The world and I look each other more calmly in the face. My mind is more self-possessed. It has done me good to be somewhat parched by the heat and drenched by the rain of life."

"Now you speak like an old philosopher," answered the Baron, laughing. "But you deceive yourself. I never knew a more restless, feverish spirit than yours. Do not think you have gained the mastery yet. You are only riding at anchor here in an eddy of the stream; you will soon be swept away again in the

mighty current and whirl of accident. Do not trust this momentary calm. I know you better than you know yourself. There is something Faust-like in you; you would fain grasp the highest and the deepest; and `reel from desire to enjoyment, and in enjoyment languish for desire.' When a momentary change of feeling comes over you, you think the change permanent, and thus live in constant self-deception."

"I confess," said Flemming, "there may be some truth in what you say. There are times when my soul is restless; and a voice sounds within me, like the trump of the archangel, and thoughts that were buried, long ago, come out of their graves. At such times my favorite occupations and pursuits no longer charm me. The quiet face of Nature seems to mock me."

"There certainly are seasons," replied the Baron, "when Nature seems not to sympathize with her beloved children. She sits there so eternally calm and self-possessed, so very motherly and serene, and cares so little whether the heart of her child breaks or not, that at times I almost lose my patience. About that, too, she cares so little, that, out of sheer obstinacy, I become good-humored again, and then she smiles."

"I think we must confess, however," continued Flemming, "that all this springs from our own imperfection, not from hers. How beautiful is this green world, which we inhabit! See yonder, how the moonlight mingles with the mist! What a glorious night is this! Truly every man has a Paradise around him until he sins, and the angel of an accusing conscience drives him from his Eden. And even then there are holy hours, when this angel sleeps, and man comes back, and, with the innocent eyes of a child, looks into his lost Paradise again,—into the broad gates and rural solitudes of Nature. I feel this often. We have much to enjoy in the quiet and retirement of our own thoughts. Boisterous mirth and loud laughter are not my mood. I love that tranquillity of soul, in which we feel the blessing of existence, and which in itself is a prayer and a thanksgiving. I find, however, that, as I grow older, I love the country less, and the city more."

"Yes," interrupted the Baron; "and presently you will love the city less and the country more. Say at once, that you have an undefined longing for both; and prefer town or country, according to the mood you are in. I think a man must be of a very quiet and happy nature, who can long endure the country; and, moreover, very well contented with his own insignificant person, very self-complacent, to be continually occupied with himself and his own thoughts. To say the least, a city life makes one more tolerant and liberal in his judgment of others. One is not eternally wrapped up in self-contemplation; which, after all, is only a more holy kind of vanity."

In conversation like this, the hours glided away; till at length, from the Giant's Tower, the Castle clock struck twelve, with a sound that seemed to come from the Middle Ages. Like watchmen from their belfries the city clocks answered it, one by one. Then distant and muffled sounds were heard. Inarticulate words seemed to blot the foggy air, as if written on wet paper. These were the bells of Handschuhsheimer, and of other villages on the broad plain of the Rhine, and among the hills of the Odenwald; mysterious sounds, that seemed not of this world.

Beneath them, in the shadow of the hills, lay the valley, like a fathomless, black gulf; and above were the cloistered stars, that, nun-like, walk the holy aisles of heaven. The city was asleep in the valley below; all asleep and silent, save the clocks, that had just struck twelve, and the veering, golden weathercocks, that were swimming in the moonshine, like golden fishes, in a glass vase. And again the wind of the summer night passed through the old Castle, and the trees, and the nightingales recorded under the dark, shadowy leaves, and the heart of Flemming was full.

When he had retired to his chamber, a feeling of utter loneliness came over him. The night before one begins a journey is always a dismal night; for, as Byron says,

"In leaving even the most unpleasant people
And places, one keeps looking at the steeple!"

And how much more so when the place and people are pleasant; as was the case with those, that Flemming was now leaving. No wonder he was sad and sleepless. Thoughts came and went, and bright and gloomy fancies, and dreams and visions, and sweet faces looked under his closed eyelids, and vanished away, and came again, and again departed. He heard the clock strike from hour to hour, and said, "Another hour is gone." At length the birds began to sing; and ever and anon the cock crew. He arose, and looked forth into the gray dawn; and before him lay the city he was so soon to leave, all white and ghastly, like a city that had arisen from its grave.

"All things must change," said he to the Baron, as he embraced him, and held him by the hand. "Friends must be torn asunder, and swept along in the current of events, to see each other seldom, and perchance no more. For ever and ever in the eddies of time and accident we whirl away. Besides which, some of us have a perpetual motion in our wooden heads, as Wodenblock had in his wooden leg; and like him we travel on, without rest or sleep, and have hardly time to take a friend by the hand in passing; and at length are seen hurrying through some distant land, worn to a skeleton, and all unknown."

BOOK III

Epigraph

"Take away the lights, too;
The moon lends me too much to find my fears;
And those devotions I am now to pay,
Are written in my heart, not in thy book;
And I shall read them there without a taper."

CHAPTER I

SUMMER-TIME

They were right,—those old German Minnesingers,—to sing the pleasant summer-time! What a time it is! How June stands illuminated in the Calendar! The windows are all wide open; only the Venetian blinds closed. Here and there a long streak of sunshine streams in through a crevice. We hear the low sound of the wind among the trees; and, as it swells and freshens, the distant doors clap to, with a sudden sound. The trees are heavy with leaves; and the gardens full of blossoms, red and white. The whole atmosphere is laden with perfume and sunshine. The birds sing. The cock struts about, and crows loftily. Insects chirp in the grass. Yellow butter-cups stud the green carpet like golden buttons, and the

red blossoms of the clover like rubies. The elm-trees reach their long, pendulous branches almost to the ground. White clouds sail aloft; and vapors fret the blue sky with silver threads. The white village gleams afar against the dark hills. Through the meadow winds the river,—careless, indolent. It seems to love the country, and is in no haste to reach the sea. The bee only is at work,—the hot and angry bee. All things else are at play; he never plays, and is vexed that any one should.

People drive out from town to breathe, and to be happy. Most of them have flowers in their hands; bunches of apple-blossoms, and still oftener lilacs. Ye denizens of the crowded city, how pleasant to you is the change from the sultry streets to the open fields, fragrant with clover-blossoms! how pleasant the fresh, breezy country air, dashed with brine from the meadows! How pleasant, above all, the flowers, the manifold, beautiful flowers!

It is no longer day. Through the trees rises the red moon, and the stars are scarcely seen. In the vast shadow of night, the coolness and the dews descend. I sit at the open window to enjoy them; and hear only the voice of the summer wind. Like black hulks, the shadows of the great trees ride at anchor on the billowy sea of grass. I cannot see the red and blue flowers, but I know that they are there. Far away in the meadow gleams the silver Charles. The tramp of horses' hoofs sounds from the wooden bridge. Then all is still, save the continuous wind of the summer night. Sometimes I know not if it be the wind or the sound of the neighbouring sea. The village clock strikes; and I feel that I am not alone.

How different is it in the city! It is late, and the crowd is gone. You step out upon the balcony, and lie in the very bosom of the cool, dewy night, as if you folded her garments about you. The whole starry heaven is spread out overhead. Beneath lies the public walk with trees, like a fathomless, black gulf, into whose silent darkness the spirit plunges and floats away, with some beloved spirit clasped in its embrace. The lamps are still burning up and down the long street. People go by, with grotesque shadows, now foreshortened and now lengthening away into the darkness and vanishing, while a new one springs up behind the walker, and seems to pass him on the sidewalk. The iron gates of the park shut with a jangling clang. There are footsteps, and loud voices;—a tumult,—a drunken brawl,—an alarm of fire;—then silence again. And now at length the city is asleep, and we can see the night. The belated moon looks over the roofs, and finds no one to welcome her. The moonlight is broken. It lies here and there in the squares, and the opening of streets,—angular, like blocks of white marble.

Under such a green, triumphal arch, O Reader! with the odor of flowers about thee, and the song of birds, shalt thou pass onward into the enchanted land, as through the Ivory Gate of dreams! And as a prelude and majestic march, one sweet human voice, I know not whose, but coming from the bosom of the Alps, sings this sublime ode, which the Alpine echoes repeat afar.

"Come, golden Evening! In the west
Enthrone the storm-dispelling sun,
And let the triple rainbow rest
O'er all the mountain tops;—'t is done;
The tempest ceases; bold and bright,
The rainbow shoots from hill to hill;
Down sinks the sun; on presses night;
Mont Blanc is lovely still!

"There take thy stand, my spirit;—spread
The world of shadows at thy feet;

And mark how calmly overhead,
The stars, like saints in glory, meet.
While, hid in solitude sublime,
Methinks I muse on Nature's tomb,
And hear the passing foot of Time
Step through the silent gloom.

"All in a moment, crash on crash,
From precipice to precipice,
An avalanche's ruins dash
Down to the nethermost abyss,
Invisible; the ear alone
Pursues the uproar till it dies;
Echo to Echo, groan for groan,
From deep to deep, replies.

"Silence again the darkness seals,
Darkness that may be felt;—but soon
The silver-clouded east reveals
The midnight spectre of the moon;
In half-eclipse she lifts her horn,
Yet, o'er the host of heaven supreme,
Brings the faint semblance of a morn,
With her awakening beam.

"Ah! at her touch, these Alpine heights
Unreal mockeries appear;
With blacker shadows, ghastlier lights,
Emerging as she climbs the sphere;
A crowd of apparitions pale!
I hold my breath in chill suspense,
They seem so exquisitely frail,
Lest they should vanish hence.

"I breathe again, I freely breathe;
Thee, Leman's Lake, once more I trace,
Like Dian's crescent far beneath,
As beautiful as Dian's face:
Pride of the land that gave me birth!
All that thy waves reflect I love,
Where heaven itself, brought down to earth,
Looks fairer than above.

"Safe on thy banks again I stray;
The trance of poesy is o'er,
And I am here at dawn of day,
Gazing on mountains as before,
Where all the strange mutations wrought,

Were magic feats of my own mind;
For, in that fairy land of thought,
Whate'er I seek, I find."

FOOT-TRAVELLING

Tell me, my soul, why art thou restless? Why dost thou look forward to the future with such strong desire? The present is thine,—and the past;—and the future shall be! O that thou didst look forward to the great hereafter with half the longing wherewith thou longest for an earthly future,—which a few days at most will bring thee! to the meeting of the dead, as to the meeting of the absent! Thou glorious spirit-land! O, that I could behold thee as thou art,—the region of life, and light, and love, and the dwelling-place of those beloved ones, whose being has flowed onward like a silver-clear stream into the solemn-sounding main, into the ocean of Eternity.

Such were the thoughts that passed through the soul of Flemming, as he lay in utter solitude and silence on the rounded summit of one of the mountains of the Furca Pass, and gazed, with tears in his eyes, and ardent longing in his heart, up into the blue-swimming heaven overhead, and at the glaciers and snowy mountain-peaks around him. Highest and whitest of all, stood the peak of the Jungfrau, which seemed near him, though it rose afar off from the bosom of the Lauterbrunner Thal. There it stood, holy and high and pure, the bride of heaven, all veiled and clothed in white, and lifted the thoughts of the beholder heavenward. O, he little thought then, as he gazed at it with longing and delight, how soon a form was to arise in his own soul, as holy, and high, and pure as this, and like this point heavenward.

Thus lay the traveller on the mountain summit, reposing his weary limbs on the short, brown grass, which more resembled moss than grass. He had sent his guide forward, that he might be alone. His soul within him was wild with a fierce and painful delight. The mountain air excited him; the mountain solitudes enticed, yet maddened him. Every peak, every sharp, jagged iceberg, seemed to pierce him. The silence was awful and sublime. It was like that in the soul of a dying man, when he hears no more the sounds of earth. He seemed to be laying aside his earthly garments. The heavens were near unto him; but between him and heaven every evil deed he had done arose gigantic, like those mountain-peaks, and breathed an icy breath upon him. O, let not the soul that suffers, dare to look Nature in the face, where she sits majestically aloft in the solitude of the mountains; for her face is hard and stern, and looks not in compassion upon her weak and erring child. It is the countenance of an accusing archangel, who summons us to judgment. In the valley she wears the countenance of a Virgin Mother, looking at us with tearful eyes, and a face of pity and love!

But yesterday Flemming had come up the valley of the Saint Gothard Pass, through Amsteg, where the Kerstelenbach comes dashing down the Maderaner Thal, from its snowy cradle overhead. The road is steep, and runs on zigzag terraces. The sides of the mountains are barren cliffs; and from their cloud-capped summits, unheard amid the roar of the great torrent below, come streams of snow white foam, leaping from rock to rock, like the mountain chamois. As you advance, the scene grows wilder and more desolate. There is not a tree in sight,—not a human habitation. Clouds, black as midnight, lower upon you from the ravines overhead; and the mountain torrent beneath is but a sheet of foam, and sends up an incessant roar. A sudden turn in the road brings you in sight of a lofty bridge, stepping from cliff to

cliff with a single stride. A fearful cataract howls beneath it, like an evil spirit, and fills the air with mist; and the mountain wind claps its hands and shrieks through the narrow pass, Ha! ha!—This is the Devil's Bridge. It leads the traveller across the fearful chasm, and through a mountain gallery into the broad, green, silent meadow of Andermath.

Even the sunny morning, which followed this gloomy day, had not chased the desolate impression from the soul of Flemming. His excitement increased as he lost himself more and more among the mountains; and now, as he lay all alone on the summit of the sunny hill, with only glaciers and snowy peaks about him, his soul, as I have said, was wild with a fierce and painful delight.

A human voice broke his reverie. He looked, and beheld at a short distance from him, the athletic form of a mountain herdsman, who was approaching the spot where he lay. He was a young man, clothed in a rustic garb, and holding a long staff in his hand. When Flemming rose, he stood still, and gazed at him, as if he loved the face of man, even in a stranger, and longed to hear a human voice, though it might speak in an unknown tongue. He answered Flemming's salutation in a rude mountain dialect, and in reply to his questions said;

"I, with two others, have charge of two hundred head of cattle on these mountains. Through the two summer months we remain here night and day; for which we receive each a Napoleon."

Flemming gave him half his summer wages. He was glad to do a good deed in secret, and yet so near heaven. The man received it as his due, like a toll-keeper; and soon after departed, leaving the traveller alone. And the traveller went his way down the mountain, as one distraught. He stopped only to pluck one bright blue flower, which bloomed all alone in the vast desert, and looked up at him, as if to say; "O take me with you! leave me not here companionless!"

Ere long he reached the magnificent glacier of the Rhone; a frozen cataract, more than two thousand feet in height, and many miles broad at its base. It fills the whole valley between two mountains, running back to their summits. At the base it is arched, like a dome; and above, jagged and rough, and resembles a mass of gigantic crystals, of a pale emerald tint, mingled with white. A snowy crust covers its surface; but at every rent and crevice the pale green ice shines clear in the sun. Its shape is that of a glove, lying with the palm downwards, and the fingers crooked and close together. It is a gauntlet of ice, which, centuries ago, Winter, the King of these mountains, threw down in defiance to the Sun; and year by year the Sun strives in vain to lift it from the ground on the point of his glittering spear. A feeling of wonder and delight came over the soul of Flemming when he beheld it, and he shouted and cried aloud;

"How wonderful! how glorious!"

After lingering a few hours in the cold, desolate valley, he climbed in the afternoon the steep Mayen-Wand, on the Grimsel, passed the Lake of the Dead, with its ink-black waters; and through the melting snow, and over slippery stepping-stones in the beds of numberless shallow brooks, descended to the Grimsel Hospital, where he passed the night, and thought it the most lone and desolate spot, that man ever slept in.

On the morrow, he rose with the day; and the rising sun found him already standing on the rustic bridge, which hangs over the verge of the Falls of the Aar at Handeck, where the river pitches down a precipice into a narrow and fearful abyss, shut in by perpendicular cliffs. At right angles with it comes the beautiful Aerlenbach; and halfway down the double cascade mingles into one. Thus he pursued his way

down the Hasli Thal into the Bernese Oberland, restless, impatient, he knew not why, stopping seldom, and never long, and then rushing forward again, like the rushing river whose steps he followed, and in whose ice-cold waters ever and anon he bathed his wrists, to cool the fever in his blood; for the noonday sun was hot.

His heart dilated in the dilating valley, that grew broader and greener at every step. The sight of human faces and human dwellings soothed him; and through the fields of summer grain, in the broad meadows of Imgrund, he walked with a heart that ached no more, but trembled only, as our eyelids when we have done weeping. As he climbed the opposite hill, which hems in this romantic valley, and, like a heavy yoke, chafes the neck of the Aar, he believed the ancient tradition, which says, that once the valley was a lake. From the summit of the hill he looked southward upon a beautiful landscape of gardens, and fields of grain, and woodlands, and meadows, and the ancient castle of Resti, looking down upon Meyringen. And now all around him were the singing of birds, and grateful shadows of the leafy trees; and sheeted waterfalls dropping from the woodland cliffs, seen only, but unheard, the fluted columns breaking into mist, and fretted with frequent spires and ornaments of foam, and not unlike the towers of a Gothic church inverted. There, in one white sheet of foam, the Riechenbach pours down into its deep beaker, into which the sun never shines. Face to face it beholds the Alpbach falling from the opposite hill, "like a downward smoke." When Flemming saw the innumerable runnels, sliding down the mountain-side, and leaping, all life and gladness, he would fain have clasped them in his arms and been their playmate, and revelled with them in their freedom and delight. Yet he was weary with the day's journey, and entered the village of Meyringen, embowered in cherry-trees, which were then laden with fruit, more like a way-worn traveller than an enthusiastic poet. As he went up the tavern steps he said in his heart, with the Italian Aretino; "He who has not been at a tavern, knows not what a paradise it is. O holy tavern! O miraculous tavern! holy, because no carking cares are there, nor weariness, nor pain; and miraculous, because of the spits, which of themselves turn round and round! Of a truth all courtesy and good manners come from taverns, so full of bows, and Signor, sì! and Signor, nò!"

But even in the tavern he could not rest long. The same evening at sunset he was floating on the lake of Brienz, in an open boat, close under the cascade of the Giessbach, hearing the peasants sing the Ranz des Vaches. He slept that night at the other extremity of the lake, in a large house, which, like Saint Peter's at Joppa, stood by the water's side. The next day he wasted in writing letters, musing in this green nest, and paddling about the lake again; and in the evening went across the beautiful meadows to Interlachen, where many things happened to him, and detained him long.

CHAPTER III

INTERLACHEN

Interlachen! How peacefully, by the margin of the swift-rushing Aar, thou liest, on the broad lap of those romantic meadows, all overshadowed by the wide arms of giant trees! Only the round towers of thine ancient cloister rise above their summits; the round towers themselves, but a child's playthings under the great church-towers of the mountains. Close beside thee are lakes, which the flowing band of the river ties together. Before thee opens the magnificent valley of Lauterbrunn, where the cloud-hooded Monk and pale Virgin stand like Saint Francis and his Bride of Snow; and all around thee are fields, and orchards, and hamlets green, from which the church-bells answer each other at evening! The evening

sun was setting when I first beheld thee! The sun of life will set ere I forget thee! Surely it was a scene like this, that inspired the soul of the Swiss poet, in his Song of the Bell!

"Bell! thou soundest merrily,
When the bridal party
To the church doth hie!
Bell! thou soundest solemnly,
When, on Sabbath morning,
Fields deserted lie!

"Bell! thou soundest merrily;
Tellest thou at evening,
Bed-time draweth nigh!
Bell! thou soundest mournfully;
Tellest thou the bitter
Parting hath gone by!

"Say! how canst thou mourn?
How canst thou rejoice?
Art but metal dull!
And yet all our sorrowings,
And all our rejoicings,
Thou dost feel them all!

"God hath wonders many,
Which we cannot fathom,
Placed within thy form!
When the heart is sinking,
Thou alone canst raise it,
Trembling in the storm!"

Paul Flemming alighted at one of the principal hotels. The landlord came out to meet him. He had great eyes and a green coat; and reminded Flemming of the innkeeper mentioned in the Golden Ass, who had been changed by magic into a frog, and croaked to his customers from the lees of a wine-cask. His house, he said, was full; and so was every house in Interlachen; but, if the gentleman would walk into the parlour, he would procure a chamber for him, in the neighbourhood.

On the sofa sat a gentleman, reading; a stout gentleman of perhaps forty-five, round, ruddy, and with a head, which, being a little bald on the top, looked not unlike a crow's nest, with one egg in it. A good-humored face turned from the book as Flemming entered; and a good-humored voice exclaimed;

"Ha! ha! Mr. Flemming! Is it you, or your apparition! I told you we should meet again! though you were for taking an eternal farewell of your fellow-traveller."

Saying these words, the stout gentleman rose and shook Flemming heartily by the hand. And Flemming returned the shake as heartily, recognising in this ruddy personage, a former travelling companion, Mr. Berkley, whom he had left, a week or two previous, toiling up the Righi. Mr. Berkley was an Englishman of fortune; a good-humored, humane old bachelor; remarkable alike for his common sense and his

eccentricity. That is to say, the basis of his character was good, sound common sense, trodden down and smoothed by education; but this level groundwork his strange and whimsical fancy used as a dancing-floor, whereon to exhibit her eccentric tricks. His ruling passion was cold-bathing; and he usually ate his breakfast sitting in a tub of cold water, and reading a newspaper. He kissed every child he met; and to every old man, said in passing, "God bless you!" with such an expression of voice and countenance, that no one could doubt his sincerity. He reminded one of Roger Bontemps, or the Little Man in Gray; though with a difference.

"The last time I had the pleasure of seeing you, Mr. Berkley," said Flemming, "was at Goldau, just as you were going up the Righi. I hope you were gratified with a fine sunrise on the mountain top."

"No, Sir, I was not!" replied Mr. Berkley. "It is all a humbug! a confounded humbug! They made such a noise about their sunrise, that I determined I would not see it. So I lay snug in bed; and only peeped through the window curtain. That was enough. Just above the house, on the top of the hill, stood some fifty half-dressed, romantic individuals, shivering in the wet grass; and, a short distance from them, a miserable wretch, blowing a long, wooden horn. That's your sunrise on the Righi, is it? said I; and went to sleep again. The best thing I saw at the Culm, was the advertisement on the bed-room doors, saying, that, if the ladies would wear the quilts and blankets for shawls, when they went out to see the sunrise, they must pay for the washing. Take my word for it, the Righi is a great humbug!"

"Where have you been since?"

"At Zurich and Schaffhausen. If you go to Zurich, beware how you stop at the Raven. They will cheat you. They cheated me; but I had my revenge, for, when we reached Schaffhausen, I wrote in the Traveller's Book;

Beware of the Raven of Zurich!
'T is a bird of omen ill;
With a noisy and an unclean nest,
And a very, very long bill.

If you go to the Golden Falken you will find it there. I am the author of those lines!"

"Bitter as Juvenal!" exclaimed Flemming.

"Not in the least bitter," said Mr. Berkley. "It is all true. Go to the Raven and see. But this Interlachen! this Interlachen! It is the loveliest spot on the face of the earth," he continued, stretching out both arms, as if to embrace the object of his affection. "There,—only look out there!"

Here he pointed to the window. Flemming looked, and beheld a scene of transcendent beauty. The plain was covered already by the brown shade of the summer twilight. From the cottage roofs in Unterseen rose here and there a thin column of smoke over the tops of the trees and mingled with the evening shadows. The Valley of Lauterbrunnen was filled with a blue haze. Far above, in the clear, cloudless heaven, the white forehead of the Jungfrau blushed at the last kiss of the departing sun. It was a glorious Transfiguration of Nature! And when the village bells began to ring, and a single voice at a great distance was heard yodling forth a ballad, it rather broke than increased the enchantment of a scene, where silence was more musical than sound.

For a long time they gazed at the gloaming landscape, and spake not. At length people came into the parlour, and laid aside their shawls and hats, and exchanged a word or two with Berkley to Flemming they were all unknown. To him it was all Mr. Brown and Mrs. Johnson, and nothing more. The conversation turned upon the various excursions of the day. Some had been at the Staubbach, others at the Grindelwald; others at the Lake of Thun; and nobody before had ever experienced half the rapture, which they had experienced that day. And thus they sat in the twilight, as people love to do, at the close of a summer day. As yet the lamps had not been lighted; and one could not distinguish faces; but voices only, and forms, like shadows.

Presently a female figure, clothed in black, entered the room and sat down by the window. She rather listened to the conversation, than joined in it; but the few words she said were spoken in a voice so musical and full of soul, that it moved the soul of Flemming, like a whisper from heaven.

O, how wonderful is the human voice! It is indeed the organ of the soul! The intellect of man sits enthroned visibly upon his forehead and in his eye; and the heart of man is written upon his countenance. But the soul reveals itself in the voice only; as God revealed himself to the prophet of old in the still, small voice; and in a voice from the burning bush. The soul of man is audible, not visible. A sound alone betrays the flowing of the eternal fountain, invisible to man!

Flemming would fain have sat and listened for hours to the sound of that unknown voice. He felt sure, in his secret heart, that the being from whom it came was beautiful. His imagination filled up the faint outline, which the eye beheld in the fading twilight, and the figure stood already in his mind, like Raphael's beautiful Madonna in the Dresden gallery. He was never more mistaken in his life. The voice belonged to a beautiful being, it is true; but her beauty was different from that of any Madonna which Raphael ever painted; as he would have seen, had he waited till the lamps were lighted. But in the midst of his reverie and saint-painting, the landlord came in, and told him he had found a chamber, which he begged him to go and look at.

Flemming took his leave and departed. Berkley went with him, to see, he said, what kind of a nest his young friend was to sleep in.

"The chamber is not what I could wish," said the landlord, as he led them across the street. "It is in the old cloister. But to-morrow or next day, you can no doubt have a room at the house."

The name of the cloister struck Flemming's imagination pleasantly. He was owl enough to like ruins and old chambers, where nuns or friars had slept. And he said to Berkley;

"So, you perceive, my nest is to be in a cloister. It already makes me think of a bird's-nest I once saw on an old tower of Heidelberg castle, built in the jaws of a lion, which formerly served as a spout. But pray tell me, who was that young lady, with the soft voice?"

"What young lady with the soft voice?"

"The young lady in black, who sat by the window."

"O, she is the daughter of an English officer, who died not long ago at Naples. She is passing the summer here with her mother, for her health."

"What is her name?"

"Ashburton."

"Is she beautiful?"

"Not in the least; but very intellectual. A woman of genius, I should say."

And now they had reached the walls of the cloister, and passed under an arched gateway, and close beneath the round towers, which Flemming had already seen, rising with their cone-shaped roofs above the trees, like tall tapers, with extinguishers upon them.

"It is not so bad, as it looks," said the landlord, knocking at a small door, in the main building. "The Bailiff lives in one part of it."

A servant girl, with a candle in her hand, opened the door, and conducted Flemming and Berkley to the chamber which had been engaged. It was a large room on the lower floor, wainscoted with pine, and unpainted. Three lofty and narrow windows, with leaden lattices and small panes, looked southward towards the valley of Lauterbrunnen and the mountains. In one corner was a large square bed, with a tester and checked curtains. In another, a huge stove of painted tiles, reaching almost to the ceiling. An old sofa, a few high-backed antique chairs, and a table, completed the furniture of the room.

Thus Flemming took possession of his monkish cell and dormitory. He ordered tea, and began to feel at home. Berkley passed the evening with him. On going away he said;

"Good night! I leave you to the care of the Virgin and all the Saints. If the ghost of any old monk comes back after his prayer-book, my compliments to him. If I were a younger man, you certainly should see a ghost. Good night!"

When he had departed, Flemming opened the lattice of one of the windows. The moon had risen, and silvered the dark outline of the nearest hills; while, afar off, the snowy summits of the Jungfrau and the Silver-Horn shone like a white cloud in the sky. Close beneath the windows was a flower-garden; and the breath of the summer night came to him with dewy fragrance. There was a grateful seclusion about the place. He blessed the happy accident, which gave him such a lodging, and fell asleep that night thinking of the nuns, who once had slept in the same quiet cells; but neither wimpled nun nor cowled monk appeared to him in his dreams; not even the face of Mary Ashburton; nor did he hear her voice.

CHAPTER IV

THE EVENING AND THE MORNING STAR

Old Froissart tells us, in his Chronicles, that when King Edward beheld the Countess of Salisbury at her castle gate, he thought he had never seen before so noble nor so fair a lady; he was stricken therewith to the heart with a sparkle of fine love, that endured long after; he thought no lady in the world so worthy to be beloved, as she. And so likewise thought Paul Flemming, when he beheld the English lady

in the fair light of a summer morning. I will not disguise the truth. She is my heroine; and I mean to describe her with great truth and beauty, so that all shall be in love with her, and I most of all.

Mary Ashburton was in her twentieth summer. Like the fair maiden Amoret, she was sitting in the lap of womanhood. They did her wrong, who said she was not beautiful; and yet

"she was not fair,
Nor beautiful;—those words express her not.
But O, her looks had something excellent,
That wants a name!"

Her face had a wonderful fascination in it. It was such a calm, quiet face, with the light of the rising soul shining so peacefully through it. At times it wore an expression of seriousness,—of sorrow even; and then seemed to make the very air bright with what the Italian poets so beautifully call the lampeggiar dell' angelico riso,—the lightning of the angelic smile.

And O, those eyes,—those deep, unutterable eyes, with "down-falling eyelids, full of dreams and slumber," and within them a cold, living light, as in mountain lakes at evening, or in the river of Paradise, forever gliding,

"with a brown, brown current
Under the shade perpetual, that never
Ray of the sun lets in, nor of the moon."

I dislike an eye that twinkles like a star. Those only are beautiful which, like the planets, have a steady, lambent light;—are luminous, but not sparkling. Such eyes the Greek poets give to the Immortals. But I forget myself.

The lady's figure was striking. Every step, every attitude was graceful, and yet lofty, as if inspired by the soul within. Angels in the old poetic philosophy have such forms; it was the soul itself imprinted on the air. And what a soul was hers! A temple dedicated to Heaven, and, like the Pantheon at Rome, lighted only from above. And earthly passions in the form of gods were no longer there, but the sweet and thoughtful faces of Christ, and the Virgin Mary, and the Saints. Thus there was not one discordant thing in her; but a perfect harmony of figure, and face, and soul, in a word of the whole being. And he who had a soul to comprehend hers, must of necessity love her, and, having once loved her, could love no other woman forevermore.

No wonder, then, that Flemming felt his heart drawn towards her, as, in her morning walk, she passed him, sitting alone under the great walnut trees near the cloister, and thinking of Heaven, but not of her. She, too, was alone. Her cheek was no longer pale; but glowing and bright, with the inspiration of the summer air. Flemming gazed after her till she disappeared, even as a vision of his dreams, he knew not whither. He was not yet in love, but very near it; for he thanked God, that he had made such beautiful beings to walk the earth.

Last night he had heard a voice to which his soul responded; and he might have gone on his way, and taken no farther heed. But he would have heard that voice afterwards, whenever at evening he thought of this evening at Interlachen. To-day he had seen more clearly the vision, and his restless soul calm. The place seemed pleasant to him; and he could not go. He did not ask himself whence came this calm. He

felt it; and was happy in the feeling; and blessed the landscape and the summer morning, as if they possessed the wonder-working power.

"A pleasant morning dream to you;" said a friendly voice; and at the same moment some one laid his hand upon Flemming's shoulder. It was Berkley. He had approached unseen and unheard.

"I see by the smile on your countenance," he continued, "that it is no day-incubus."

"You are right," replied Flemming. "It was a pleasant dream, which you have put to flight."

"And I am glad to see, that you have also put to flight the gloomy thoughts which used to haunt you. I like to see people cheerful and happy. What is the use of giving way to sadness in this beautiful world?"

"Ah! this beautiful world!" said Flemming, with a smile. "Indeed, I know not what to think of it. Sometimes it is all gladness and sunshine, and Heaven itself lies not far off. And then it changes suddenly; and is dark and sorrowful, and clouds shut out the sky. In the lives of the saddest of us, there are bright days like this, when we feel as if we could take the great world in our arms and kiss it. Then come the gloomy hours, when the fire will neither burn on our hearths nor in our hearts; and all without and within is dismal, cold, and dark. Believe me, every heart has its secret sorrows, which the world knows not, and oftentimes we call a man cold, when he is only sad."

"And who says we don't?" interrupted Berkley. "Come, come! Let us go to breakfast. The morning air has given me a rude appetite. I long to say grace over a fresh egg; and eat salt with my worst enemies; namely, the Cockneys at the hotel. After breakfast you must give yourself up wholly to me. I shall take you to the Grindelwald!"

"To-day, then, you do not breakfast like Diogenes, but consent to leave your tub."

"Yes, for the pleasure of your company. I shall also blow out the light in my lantern, having found you."

"Thank you."

The breakfast passed without any unusual occurrence. Flemming watched the entrance of every guest; but she came not,—the guest he most desired to see.

"And now for the Grindelwald!" said Berkley.

"Why such haste? We have the whole day before us. There is time enough."

"Not a moment to lose, I assure you. The carriage is at the door."

They drove up the valley of Lauterbrunnen, and turned eastward among the mountains of the Grindelwald. There they passed the day; half-frozen by the icy breath of the Great Glacier, upon whose surface stand pyramids and blocks of ice, like the tombstones of a cemetery. It was a weary day to Flemming. He wished himself at Interlachen; and was glad when, towards evening, he saw once more the cone-roofed towers of the cloister rising above the walnut trees.

That evening is written in red letters in his history. It gave him another revelation of the beauty and excellence of the female character and intellect; not wholly new to him, yet now renewed and fortified. It was from the lips of Mary Ashburton, that the revelation came. Her form arose, like a tremulous evening star, in the firmament of his soul. He conversed with her; and with her alone; and knew not when to go. All others were to him as if they were not there. He saw their forms, but saw them as the forms of inanimate things. At length her mother came; and Flemming beheld in her but another Mary Ashburton, with beauty more mature;—the same forehead and eyes, the same majestic figure; and, as yet, no trace of age. He gazed upon her with a feeling of delight, not unmingled with holy awe. She was to him the rich and glowing Evening, from whose bosom the tremulous star was born.

Berkley took no active part in the conversation, but did what was much more to the purpose, that it is to say, arranged a drive for the next day with the Ashburtons, and of course invited Flemming, who went home that night with a halo round his head; and wondering much at a dandy, who stood at the door of the hotel, and said to his companion, as Flemming passed;

"What do you call this place? I have been here two hours already, and find it devilish dull!"

CHAPTER V

A RAINY DAY

When Flemming awoke the next morning he saw the sky dark and lowering. From the mountain tops hung a curtain of mist, whose heavy folds waved to and fro in the valley below. Over all the landscape, the soft, summer rain was falling. No admiring eyes would look up that day at the Staubbach.

A rainy day in Switzerland puts a sudden stop to many diversions. The coachman may drive to the tavern and then back to the stable; but no farther. The sunburnt guide may sit at the ale-house door, and welcome; and the boatman whistle and curse the clouds, at his own sweet will; but no foot stirs abroad for all that; no traveller moves, if he has time to stay. The rainy day gives him time for reflection. He has leisure now to take cognizance of his impressions, and make up his account with the mountains. He remembers, too, that he has friends at home; and writes up the Journal, neglected for a week or more; and letters neglected longer; or finishes the rough pencil-sketch, begun yesterday in the open air. On the whole he is not sorry it rains; though disappointed.

Flemming was both sorry and disappointed; but he did not on that account fail to go over to the Ashburtons at the appointed hour. He found them sitting in the parlour. The mother was reading, and the daughter retouching a sketch of the Lake of Thun. After the usual salutations, Flemming seated himself near the daughter, and said;

"We shall have no Staubbach to-day, I presume; only this Giessbach from the clouds."

"Nothing more, I suppose. So we must be content to stay in-doors; and listen to the sound of the eves-dropping rain. It gives me time to finish some of these rough sketches."

"It is a pleasant pastime," said Flemming; "and I perceive you are very skilful. I am delighted to see, that you can draw a straight line. I never before saw a lady's sketch-book, in which all the towers did not resemble the leaning Tower of Pisa. I always tremble for the little men under them."

"How absurd!" exclaimed Mary Ashburton, with a smile that passed through the misty air of Flemming's thoughts, like a sunbeam; "For one, I succeed much better in straight lines than in any others. Here I have been trying a half-hour to make this water-wheel round; and round it never will be."

"Then let it remain as it is. It looks uncommonly picturesque, and may pass for a new invention."

The lady continued to sketch, and Flemming to gaze at her beautiful face; often repeating to himself those lines in Marlow's Faust;

"O thou art fairer than the evening air,
Clad in the beauty of a thousand stars!"

He certainly would have betrayed himself to the maternal eye of Mrs. Ashburton, had she not been wholly absorbed in the follies of a fashionable novel. Ere long the fair sketcher had paused for a moment; and Flemming had taken her sketch-book in his hands and was looking it through from the beginning with ever-increasing delight, half of which he dared not express, though he favored her with some comments and bursts of admiration.

"This is truly a very beautiful sketch of Murten and the battle-field! How quietly the land-scape sleeps there by the lake, after the battle! Did you ever read the ballad of Veit Weber, the shoe-maker, on this subject? He says, the routed Burgundians jumped into the lake, and the Swiss Leaguers shot them down like wild ducks among the reeds. He fought in the battle and wrote the ballad afterwards;—

'He had himself laid hand on sword,
He who this rhyme did write;
Till evening mowed he with the sword,
And sang the song at night.'"

"You must give me the whole ballad," said Miss Ashburton; "it will serve to illustrate the sketch."

"And the sketch to illustrate the ballad. And now we suddenly slide down the Alps into Italy, and are even in Rome, if I mistake not. This is surely a head of Homer?"

"Yes," replied the lady, with a little enthusiasm. "Do you not remember the marble bust at Rome? When I first beheld that bust, it absolutely inspired me with awe. It is not the face of a man, but of a god!"

"And you have done it no injustice in your copy," said Flemming, catching a new enthusiasm from hers. "With what a classic grace the fillet, passing round the majestic forehead, confines his flowing locks, which mingle with his beard! The countenance, too, is calm, majestic, godlike! Even the fixed and sightless eyeballs do not mar the image of the seer! Such were the sightless eyes of the blind old man of Chios. They seem to look with mournful solemnity into the mysterious future; and the marble lips to repeat that prophetic passage in the Hymn to Apollo; 'Let me also hope to be remembered in ages to come. And when any one, born of the tribes of men, comes hither, a weary traveller, and inquires, who is the sweetest of the Singing Men, that resort to your feasts, and whom you most delight to hear, do

you make answer for me. It is the Blind Man, who dwells in Chios; his songs excel all that can ever be sung!' But do you really believe, that this is a portrait of Homer?"

"Certainly not! It is only an artist's dream. It was thus, that Homer appeared to him in his visions of the antique world. Every one, you know, forms an image in his fancy of persons and things he has never seen; and the artist reproduces them in marble or on canvass."

"And what is the image in your fancy? Is it like this?"

"No; not entirely. I have drawn my impressions from another source. Whenever I think of Homer, which is not often, he walks before me, solemn and serene, as in the vision of the great Italian; in countenance neither sorrowful nor glad, followed by other bards, and holding in his right hand a sword!"

"That is a finer conception, than even this," said Flemming. "And I perceive from your words, as well as from this book, that you have a true feeling for art, and understand what it is. You have had bright glimpses into the enchanted land."

"I trust," replied the lady modestly, "that I am not wholly without this feeling. Certainly I have as strong and passionate a love of Art as of Nature."

"But does it not often offend you to hear people speaking of Art and Nature as opposite and discordant things? Surely nothing can be more false. Nature is a revelation of God; Art a revelation of man. Indeed, Art signifies no more than this. Art is Power. That is the original meaning of the word. It is the creative power by which the soul of man makes itself known, through some external manifestation or outward sign. As we can always hear the voice of God, walking in the garden, in the cool of the day, or under the star-light, where, to quote one of this poet's verses, 'high prospects and the brows of all steep hills and pinnacles thrust up themselves for shows';—so, under the twilight and the starlight of past ages, do we hear the voice of man, walking amid the works of his hands, and city walls and towers and the spires of churches, thrust up themselves for shows."

The lady smiled at his warmth; and he continued;

"This, however, is but a similitude; and Art and Nature are more nearly allied than by similitudes only. Art is the revelation of man; and not merely that, but likewise the revelation of Nature, speaking through man. Art pre-ëxists in Nature, and Nature is reproduced in Art. As vapors from the ocean, floating landward and dissolved in rain, are carried back in rivers to the ocean, so thoughts and the semblances of things that fall upon the soul of man in showers, flow out again in living streams of Art, and lose themselves in the great ocean, which is Nature. Art and Nature are not, then, discordant, but ever harmoniously working in each other."

Enthusiasm begets enthusiasm. Flemming spake with such evident interest in the subject, that Miss Ashburton did not fail to manifest some interest in what he said; and, encouraged by this, he proceeded;

"Thus in this wondrous world wherein we live, which is the World of Nature, man has made unto himself another world hardly less wondrous, which is the World of Art. And it lies infolded and compassed about by the other,

'And the clear region where 't was born,

Round in itself incloses.'

Taking this view of art, I think we understand more easily the skill of the artist, and the difference between him and the mere amateur. What we call miracles and wonders of art are not so to him who created them. For they were created by the natural movements of his own great soul. Statues, paintings, churches, poems, are but shadows of himself;—shadows in marble, colors, stone, words. He feels and recognises their beauty; but he thought these thoughts and produced these things as easily as inferior minds do thoughts and things inferior. Perhaps more easily. Vague images and shapes of beauty floating through the soul, the semblances of things as yet indefinite or ill-defined, and perfect only when put in art,—this Possible Intellect, as the Scholastic Philosophers have termed it,—the artist shares in common with us all. The lovers of art are many. But the Active Intellect, the creative power,—the power to put these shapes and images in art, to imbody the indefinite, and render perfect, is his alone. He shares the gift with few. He knows not even whence nor how this is. He knows only that it is; that God has given him the power, which has been denied to others."

"I should have known you were just from Germany," said the lady, with a smile, "even if you had not told me so. You are an enthusiast for the Germans. For my part I cannot endure their harsh language."

"You would like it better, if you knew it better," answered Flemming. "It is not harsh to me; but homelike, hearty, and full of feeling, like the sound of happy voices at a fireside, of a winter's night, when the wind blows, and the fire crackles, and hisses, and snaps. I do indeed love the Germans; the men are so hale and hearty, and the Fräuleins so tender and true!"

"I always think of men with pipes and beer, and women with knitting work."

"O, those are English prejudices," exclaimed Flemming. "Nothing can be more—"

"And their very literature presents itself to my imagination under the same forms."

"I see you have read only English criticisms; and have an idea, that all German books smell, as it were, 'of groceries, of brown papers, filled with greasy cakes and slices of bacon; and of fryings in frowzy back-parlours; and this shuts you out from a glorious world of poetry, romance, and dreams!"

Mary Ashburton smiled, and Flemming continued to turn over the leaves of the sketch-book, with an occasional criticism and witticism. At length he came to a leaf which was written in pencil. People of a lively imagination are generally curious, and always so when a little in love.

"Here is a pencil-sketch," said he, with an entreating look, "which I would fain examine with the rest."

"You may do so, if you wish; but you will find it the poorest sketch in the book. I was trying one day to draw the picture of an artist's life in Rome, as it presented itself to my imagination; and this is the result. Perhaps it may awaken some pleasant recollection in your mind."

Flemming waited no longer; but read with the eyes of a lover, not of a critic, the following description, which inspired him with a new enthusiasm for Art, and for Mary Ashburton.

"I often reflect with delight upon the young artist's life in Rome. A stranger from the cold and gloomy North, he has crossed the Alps, and with the devotion of a pilgrim journeyed to the Eternal City. He

dwells perhaps upon the Pincian Hill; and hardly a house there, which is not inhabited by artists from foreign lands. The very room he lives in has been their abode from time out of mind. Their names are written all over the walls; perhaps some further record of them left in a rough sketch upon the window-shutter, with an inscription and a date. These things consecrate the place, in his imagination. Even these names, though unknown to him, are not without associations in his mind.

"In that warm latitude he rises with the day. The night-vapors are already rolling away over the Campagna sea-ward. As he looks from his window, above and beyond their white folds he recognises the tremulous blue sea at Ostia. Over Soracte rises the sun,—over his own beloved mountain; though no longer worshipped there, as of old. Before him, the antique house, where Raphael lived, casts its long, brown shadow down into the heart of modern Rome. The city lies still asleep and silent. But above its dark roofs, more than two hundred steeples catch the sunshine on their gilded weather-cocks. Presently the bells begin to ring, and, as the artist listens to their pleasant chimes, he knows that in each of those churches over the high altar, hangs a painting by some great master's hand, whose beauty comes between him and heaven, so that he cannot pray, but wonder only.

"Among these works of art he passes the day; but oftenest in St. Peter's and the Vatican. Up the vast marble stair-case,—through the Corridor Chiaramonti,—through vestibules, galleries, chambers,—he passes, as in a dream. All are filled with busts and statues; or painted in daring frescoes. What forms of strength and beauty! what glorious creations of the human mind! and in that last chamber of all, standing alone upon his pedestal, the Apollo found at Actium,—in such a majestic attitude,—with such a noble countenance, life-like, god-like!

"Or perhaps he passes into the chambers of the painters; but goes no further than the second. For in the middle of that chamber a large painting stands upon the heavy easel, as if unfinished, though more than three hundred years ago the great artist completed it, and then laid his pencil away forever, leaving this last benediction to the world. It is the Transfiguration of Christ by Raphael. A child looks not at the stars with greater wonder, than the artist at this painting. He knows how many studious years are in that picture. He knows the difficult path that leads to perfection, having himself taken some of the first steps.—Thus he recalls the hour, when that broad canvass was first stretched upon its frame, and Raphael stood before it, and laid the first colors upon it, and beheld the figures one by one born into life, and 'looked upon the work of his own hands with a smile, that it should have succeeded so well.' He recalls too, the hour, when, the task accomplished, the pencil dropped from the master's dying hand, and his eyes closed to open on a more glorious transfiguration, and at length the dead Raphael lay in his own studio, before this wonderful painting, more glorious than any conqueror under the banners and armorial hatchments of his funeral!

"Think you, that such sights and thoughts as these do not move the heart of a young man and an artist! And when he goes forth into the open air, the sun is going down, and the gray ruins of an antique world receive him. From the Palace of the Cæsars he looks down into the Forum, or towards the Coliseum; or westward sees the last sunshine strike the bronze Archangel, which stands upon the Tomb of Adrian. He walks amid a world of Art in ruins. The very street-lamps, that light him homeward, burn before some painted or sculptured image of the Madonna! What wonder is it, if dreams visit him in his sleep,—nay, if his whole life seem to him a dream! What wonder, if, with a feverish heart and quick hand, he strive to reproduce those dreams in marble or on canvass."

Foolish Paul Flemming! who both admired and praised this little sketch, and yet was too blind to see, that it was written from the heart, and not from the imagination! Foolish Paul Flemming! who thought,

that a girl of twenty could write thus, without a reason! Close upon this followed another pencil sketch, which he likewise read, with the lady's permission. It was this.

"The whole period of the Middle Ages seems very strange to me. At times I cannot persuade myself that such things could have been, as history tells us; that such a strange world was a part of our world,—that such a strange life was a part of the life, which seems to us who are living it now, so passionless and commonplace. It is only when I stand amid ruined castles, that look at me so mournfully, and behold the heavy armour of old knights, hanging upon the wainscot of Gothic chambers; or when I walk amid the aisles of some dusky minster, whose walls are narrative of hoar antiquity, and whose very bells have been baptized, and see the carved oaken stalls in the choir, where so many generations of monks have sat and sung, and the tombs, where now they sleep in silence, to awake no more to their midnight psalms;—it is only at such times, that the history of the Middle Ages is a reality to me, and not a passage in romance.

"Likewise the illuminated manuscripts of those ages have something of this power of making the dead Past a living Present in my mind. What curious figures are emblazoned on the creaking parchment, making its yellow leaves laugh with gay colors! You seem to come upon them unawares. Their faces have an expression of wonder. They seem all to be just startled from their sleep by the sound you made when you unloosed the brazen clasps, and opened the curiously-carved oaken covers, that turn on hinges, like the great gates of a city. To the building of that city some diligent monk gave the whole of a long life. With what strange denizens he peopled it! Adam and Eve standing under a tree, she, with the apple in her hand;—the patriarch Abraham, with a tree growing out of his body, and his descendants sitting owl-like upon its branches;—ladies with flowing locks of gold; knights in armour, with most fantastic, long-toed shoes; jousts and tournaments; and Minnesingers, and lovers, whose heads reach to the towers, where their ladies sit;—and all so angular, so simple, so childlike,—all in such simple attitudes, with such great eyes, and holding up such long, lank fingers!—These things are characteristic of the Middle Ages, and persuade me of the truth of history."

At this moment Berkley entered, with a Swiss cottage, which he had just bought as a present for somebody's child in England; and a cane with a chamois-horn on the end of it, which he had just bought for himself. This was the first time, that Flemming had been sorry to see the good-natured man. His presence interrupted the delightful conversation he was carrying on "under four eyes," with Mary Ashburton. He really thought Berkley a bore, and wondered it had never occurred to him before. Mrs. Ashburton, too, must needs lay down her book; and the conversation became general. Strange to say, the Swiss dinner-hour of one o'clock, did not come a moment too soon for Flemming. It did not even occur to him that it was early; for he was seated beside Mary Ashburton, and at dinner one can say so much, without being overheard.

CHAPTER VI

AFTER DINNER, AND AFTER THE MANNER OF THE BEST CRITICS

When the learned Thomas Diafoirus wooed the fair Angélique, he drew from his pocket a medical thesis, and presented it to her, as the first-fruits of his genius; and at the same time, invited her, with her father's permission, to attend the dissection of a woman, upon whom he was to lecture. Paul Flemming did nearly the same thing; and so often, that it had become a habit. He was continually drawing, from

his pocket or his memory, some scrap of song or story; and inviting some fair Angélique, either with her father's permission or without, to attend the dissection of an author, upon whom he was to discourse. He soon gave proofs of this to Mary Ashburton.

"What books have we here for afternoon reading?" said Flemming, taking a volume from the parlour table, when they had returned from the dining-room. "O, it is Uhland's Poems. Have you read any thing of his? He and Tieck are the best living poets of Germany. They dispute the palm of superiority. Let me give you a lesson in German, this afternoon, Miss Ashburton; so that no one may accuse you of 'omitting the sweet benefit of time, to clothe your age with angel-like perfection.' I have opened at random upon the ballad of the Black Knight. You repeat the German after me, and I will translate to you. Pfingsten war, das Fest der Freude!"

"I should never persuade my unwilling lips to pronounce such sounds. So I beg you not to perplex me with your German, but read me the ballad in English."

"Well, then, listen. I will improvise a translation for your own particular benefit.

"'T was Pentecost, the Feast of Gladness,
When woods and fields put off all sadness.
Thus began the King and spake;
'So from the halls
Of ancient Hofburg's walls,
A luxuriant Spring shall break.'

"Drums and trumpets echo loudly,
Wave the crimson banners proudly.
From balcony the King looked on;
In the play of spears,
Fell all the cavaliers,
Before the monarch's stalwart son.

"To the barrier of the fight,
Rode at last a sable Knight.
'Sir Knight! your name and scutcheon, say!'
'Should I speak it here,
Ye would stand aghast with fear;
Am a Prince of mighty sway!'

"When he rode into the lists,
The arch of heaven grew black with mists,
And the castle 'gan to rock.
At the first blow,
Fell the youth from saddle-bow,
Hardly rises from the shock.

"Pipe and viol call the dances,
Torch-light through the high halls glances;
Waves a mighty shadow in.

With manner bland
Doth ask the maiden's hand,
Doth with her the dance begin.

"Danced in sable iron sark,
Danced a measure weird and dark,
Coldly clasped her limbs around.
From breast and hair
Down fall from her the fair
Flowerets wilted to the ground.

"To the sumptuous banquet came
Every Knight and every Dame.
'Twixt son and daughter all distraught,
With mournful mind
The ancient King reclined,
Gazed at them in silent thought.

"Pale the children both did look,
But the guest a beaker took;
'Golden wine will make you whole!"
The children drank,
Gave many a courteous thank;
'O that draught was very cool!'

"Each the father's breast embraces,
Son and daughter; and their faces
Colorless grow utterly.
Whichever way
Looks the fear-struck father gray,
He beholds his children die.

"'Woe! the blessed children both,
Takest thou in the joy of youth;
Take me, too, the joyless father!'
Spake the Grim Guest,
From his hollow, cavernous breast;
'Roses in the spring I gather!'"

"That is indeed a striking ballad!" said Miss Ashburton, "but rather too grim and ghostly for this dull afternoon."

"It begins joyously enough with the feast of Pentecost, and the crimson banners at the old castle. Then the contrast is well managed. The Knight in black mail, and the waving in of the mighty shadow in the dance, and the dropping of the faded flowers, are all strikingly presented to the imagination. However, it tells its own story, and needs no explanation. Here is something in a different vein, though still melancholy. The Castle by the Sea. Shall I read it?"

"Yes, if you like."

Flemming read;

"Hast thou seen that lordly castle,
That Castle by the Sea?
Golden and red above it
The clouds float gorgeously.

"And fain it would stoop downward
To the mirrored wave below;
And fain it would soar upward
In the evening's crimson glow.

"'Well have I seen that castle,
That Castle by the Sea,
And the moon above it standing,
And the mist rise solemnly.'

"The winds and the waves of ocean,
Had they a merry chime?
Didst thou hear, from those lofty chambers,
The harp and the minstrel's rhyme?

" 'The winds and the waves of ocean,
They rested quietly,
But I heard on the gale a sound of wail,
And tears came to my eye.'

"And sawest thou on the turrets
The King and his royal bride?
And the wave of their crimson mantles?
And the golden crown of pride?

"Led they not forth in rapture
A beauteous maiden there?
Resplendent as the morning sun,
Beaming with golden hair?

" 'Well saw I the ancient parents,
Without the crown of pride;
They were moving slow, in weeds of woe,
No maiden was by their side!'
How do you like that?"

"It is very graceful, and pretty. But Uhland seems to leave a great deal to his reader's imagination. All his readers should be poets themselves, or they will hardly comprehend him. I confess, I hardly understand the passage where he speaks of the castle's stooping downward to the mirrored wave below, and then

soaring upward into the gleaming sky. I suppose, however, he wishes to express the momentary illusion we experience at beholding a perfect reflection of an old tower in the sea, and look at it as if it were not a mere shadow in the water; and yet the real tower rises far above, and seems to float in the crimson evening clouds. Is that the meaning?"

"I should think it was. To me it is all a beautiful cloud landscape, which I comprehend and feel, and yet should find some difficulty perhaps in explaining."

"And why need one always explain? Some feelings are quite untranslatable. No language has yet been found for them. They gleam upon us beautifully through the dim twilight of fancy, and yet, when we bring them close to us, and hold them up to the light of reason, lose their beauty, all at once; just as glow-worms, which gleam with such a spiritual light in the shadows of evening, when brought in where the candles are lighted, are found to be only worms, like so many others."

"Very true. We ought sometimes to be content with feeling. Here, now, is an exquisite piece, which soothes one like the fall of evening shadows,—like the dewy coolness of twilight after a sultry day. I shall not give you a bald translation of my own, because I have laid up in my memory another, which, though not very literal, equals the original in beauty. Observe how finely it commences.

"Many a year is in its grave,
Since I crossed this restless wave;
And the evening, fair as ever,
Shines on ruin, rock, and river.

"Then, in this same boat, beside,
Sat two comrades old and tried;
One with all a father's truth,
One with all the fire of youth.

"One on earth in silence wrought,
And his grave in silence sought;
But the younger, brighter form
Passed in battle and in storm!

"So, whene'er I turn my eye
Back upon the days gone by,
Saddening thoughts of friends come o'er me,—
Friends, who closed their course before me.

"Yet what binds us, friend to friend,
But that soul with soul can blend?
Soul-like were those hours of yore;
Let us walk in soul once more!

"Take, O boatman, thrice thy fee;
Take,—I give it willingly;
For, invisibly to thee,
Spirits twain have crossed with me!"

"O, that is beautiful,—'beautiful exceedingly!' Who translated it?"

"I do not know. I wish I could find him out. It is certainly admirably done; though in the measure of the original there is something like the rocking motion of a boat, which is not preserved in the translation."

"And is Uhland always so soothing and spiritual?"

"Yes, he generally looks into the spirit-world. I am now trying to find here a little poem on the Death of a Country Clergyman; in which he introduces a beautiful picture. But I cannot turn to it. No matter. He describes the spirit of the good old man, returning to earth on a bright summer morning, and standing amid the golden corn and the red and blue flowers, and mildly greeting the reapers as of old. The idea is beautiful, is it not?"

"Yes, very beautiful!"

"But there is nothing morbid in Uhland's mind. He is always fresh and invigorating, like a breezy morning. In this he differs entirely from such writers as Salis and Matthisson."

"And who are they?"

"Two melancholy gentlemen to whom life was only a Dismal Swamp, upon whose margin they walked with cambric handkerchiefs in their hands, sobbing and sighing, and making signals to Death, to come and ferry them over the lake. And now their spirits stand in the green fields of German song, like two weeping-willows, bending over a grave. To read their poems, is like wandering through a village churchyard on a summer evening, reading the inscription upon the grave-stones, and recalling sweet images of the departed; while above you,

'Hark! in the holy grove of palms,
Where the stream of life runs free,
Echoes, in the angels' psalms,
'Sister spirit! hail to thee!'"

"How musically those lines flow! Are they Matthisson's!"

"Yes; and they do indeed flow musically. I wish I had his poems here. I should like to read to you his Elegy on the Ruins of an Ancient Castle. It is an imitation of Gray's Elegy. You have been at Baden-Baden?

"Yes; last summer."

"And have not forgotten—"

"The old castle? Of course not. What a magnificent ruin it is!"

"That is the scene of Matthisson's Poem, and seems to have filled the melancholy bard with more than wonted inspiration."

"I should like very much to see the poem, I remember that old ruin with so much delight."

"I am sorry I have not a translation of it for you. Instead of it I will give you a sweet and mournful poem from Salis. It is called the Song of the Silent Land.

"Into the Silent Land!
Ah! who shall lead us thither!
Clouds in the evening sky more darkly gather,
And shattered wrecks lie thicker on the strand.
Who leads us with a gentle hand,
Thither, oh, thither.
Into the Silent Land?

"Into the Silent Land!
To you, ye boundless regions
Of all perfection! Tender morning-visions
Of beauteous souls! Eternity's own band!
Who in Life's battle firm doth stand,
Shall bear Hope's tender blossoms
Into the Silent Land!

"O Land! O Land!
For all the broken-hearted
The mildest herald by our fate allotted,
Beckons, and with inverted torch doth stand
To lead us with a gentle hand
Into the land of the great departed,
Into the Silent Land!
Is not that a beautiful poem?"

Mary Ashburton made no answer. She had turned away to hide her tears. Flemming wondered, that Berkley could say she was not beautiful. Still he was rather pleased than offended at it. He felt at that moment how sweet a thing it would be to possess one, who should seem beautiful to him alone, and yet to him be more beautiful than all the world beside! How bright the world became to him at that thought! It was like one of those paintings in which all the light streams from the face of the Virgin. O, there is nothing holier in this life of ours, than the first consciousness of love,—the first fluttering of its silken wings; the first rising sound and breath of that wind, which is so soon to sweep through the soul, to purify or to destroy!

Old histories tell us, that the great Emperor Charlemagne stamped his edicts with the hilt of his sword. The greater Emperor, Death, stamps his with the blade; and they are signed and executed with the same stroke. Flemming received that night a letter from Heidelberg, which told him, that Emma of Ilmenau was dead. The fate of this poor girl affected him deeply; and he said in his heart;

"Father in Heaven! Why was the lot of this weak and erring child so hard! What had she done, to be so tempted in her weakness, and perish? Why didst thou suffer her gentle affections to lead her thus astray?"

And, through the silence of the awful midnight, the voice of an avalanche answered from the distant mountains, and seemed to say;

"Peace! peace! Why dost thou question God's providence!"

TAKE CARE!

Fair is the valley of Lauterbrunnen with its green meadows and overhanging cliffs. The ruined castle of Unspunnen stands like an armed warder at the gate of the enchanted land. In calm serenity the snowy mountains rise beyond. Fairer than the Rock of Balmarusa, you frowning precipice looks down upon us; and, from the topmost cliff, the white pennon of the Brook of Dust shimmers and waves in the sunny air!

It was a bright, beautiful morning after night rain. Every dewdrop and raindrop had a whole heaven within it; and so had the heart of Paul Flemming, as, with Mrs. Ashburton and her dark-eyed daughter, he drove up the Valley of Lauter-brunnen,—the Valley of Fountains-Only.

"How beautiful the Jungfrau looks this morning!" exclaimed he, looking at Mary Ashburton.

She thought he meant the mountain, and assented. But he meant her likewise.

"And the mountains, beyond," he continued; "the Monk and the Silver-horn, the Wetter-horn the Schreck-horn, and the Schwarz-horn, all those sublime apostles of Nature, whose sermons are avalanches! Did you ever behold anything more grand!"

"O yes. Mont Blanc is more grand, when you behold it from the hills opposite. It was there that I was most moved by the magnificence of Swiss scenery. It was a morning like this; and the clouds, that were hovering about on their huge, shadowy wings, made the scene only the more magnificent. Before me lay the whole panorama of the Alps; pine forests standing dark and solemn at the base of the mountains; and half-way up a veil of mist; above which rose the snowy summits, and sharp needles of rock, which seemed to float in the air, like a fairy world. Then the glaciers stood on either side, winding down through the mountain ravines; and, high above all, rose the white, dome-like summit of Mont Blanc. And ever and anon from the shroud of mist came the awful sound of an avalanche, and a continual roar, as of the wind through a forest of pines, filled the air. It was the roar of the Arve and Aveiron, breaking from their icy fountains. Then the mists began to pass away; and it seemed as if the whole firmament were rolling together. It recalled to my mind that sublime passage in the Apocalypse; 'I saw a great white throne; and him that sat thereon; before whose face the heavens and the earth fled away, and found no place!' O, I cannot believe that upon this earth there is a more magnificent scene."

"It must be grand, indeed," replied Flemming. "And those mighty glaciers,—huge monsters with bristling crests, creeping down into the valley! for it is said they really move."

"Yes; it filled me with a strange sensation of awe to think of this. They seemed to me like the dragons of Northern Romance, which come down from the mountains and devour whole villages. A little hamlet in

Chamouni was once abandoned by its inhabitants, terrified at the approach of the icy dragon. But is it possible you have never been at Chamouni?

"Never. The great marvel still remains unseen by me."

"Then how can you linger here so long? Were I in your place I would not lose an hour."

These words passed over the opening blossoms of hope in the soul of Flemming, like a cold wind over the flowers in spring-time. He bore it as best he could, and changed the subject.

I do not mean to describe the Valley of Lauterbrunnen, nor the bright day passed there. I know that my gentle reader is blessed with the divine gift of a poetic fancy; and can see already how the mountains rise, and the torrents fall, and the sweet valley lies between; and how, along the dusty road, the herdsman blows his horn, and travellers come and go in charabans, like Punch and Judy in a show-box. He knows already how romantic ladies sketch romantic scenes; while sweet gentlemen gather sweet flowers; and how cold meat tastes under the shadow of trees, and how time flies when we are in love, and the beloved one near. One little incident I must, however, mention, lest his fancy should not suggest it.

Flemming was still sitting with the ladies, on the green slope near the Staubbach, or Brook of Dust, when a young man clad in green, came down the valley. It was a German student, with flaxen ringlets hanging over his shoulders, and a guitar in his hand. His step was free and elastic, and his countenance wore the joyous expression of youth and health. He approached the company with a courteous salutation; and, after the manner of travelling students, asked charity with the confident air of one unaccustomed to refusal. Nor was he refused in this instance. The presence of those we love makes us compassionate and generous. Flemming gave him a piece of gold; and after a short conversation he seated himself, at a little distance on the grass, and began to play and sing. Wonderful and many were the sweet accords and plaintive sounds that came from that little instrument, touched by the student's hand. Every feeling of the human heart seemed to find an expression there, and awaken a kindred feeling in the hearts of those who heard him. He sang sweet German songs, so full of longing, and of pleasing sadness, and hope and fear, and passionate desire, and soul-subduing sorrow, that the tears came into Mary Ashburton's eyes, though she understood not the words he sang. Then his countenance glowed with triumph, and he beat the strings like a drum, and sang;

"O, how the drum beats so loud!
Close beside me in the fight,
My dying brother says, Good Night!
And the cannon's awful breath
Screams the loud halloo of Death!
And the drum,
And the drum,
Beats so loud!"

Many were the words of praise, when the young musician ended; and, as he rose to depart, they still entreated for one song more. Whereupon he played a lively prelude; and, looking full into Flemming's face, sang with a pleasant smile, and still in German, this little song.

"I KNOW a maiden fair to see,

Take care!
She can both false and friendly be,
Beware! Beware!
Trust her not,
She is fooling thee!

"She has two eyes, so soft and brown,
Take care!
She gives a side-glance and looks down,
Beware! Beware!
Trust her not,
She is fooling thee!

"And she has hair of a golden hue,
Take care!
And what she says, it is not true,
Beware! Beware!
Trust her not,
She is fooling thee!

"She has a bosom as white as snow,
Take care!
She knows how much it is best to show,
Beware! Beware!
Trust her not,
She is fooling thee!

"She gives thee a garland woven fair,
Take care!
It is a fool's cap for thee to wear,
Beware! Beware!
Trust her not,
She is fooling thee!"

The last stanza he sung in a laughing, triumphant tone, which resounded above the loud clang of his guitar, like the jeering laugh of Till Eulenspiegel. Then slinging his guitar over his shoulder, he took off his green cap, and made a leg to the ladies, in the style of Gil Blas; waved his hand in the air, and walked quickly down the valley, singing "Adé! Adé! Adé!"

CHAPTER VIII

THE FOUNTAIN OF OBLIVION

The power of magic in the Middle Ages created monsters, who followed the unhappy magician everywhere. The power of Love in all ages creates angels, who likewise follow the happy or unhappy lover everywhere, even in his dreams. By such an angel was Paul Flemming now haunted, both when he

waked and when he slept. He walked as in a dream; and was hardly conscious of the presence of those around him. A sweet face looked at him from every page of every book he read; and it was the face of Mary Ashburton! a sweet voice spake to him in every sound he heard; and it was the voice of Mary Ashburton! Day and night succeeded each other, with pleasant interchange of light and darkness; but to him the passing of time was only as a dream. When he arose in the morning, he thought only of her, and wondered if she were yet awake; and when he lay down at night he thought only of her, and how, like the Lady Christabel,

"Her gentle limbs she did undress,
And lay down in her loveliness."

And the livelong day he was with her, either in reality or in day-dreams, hardly less real; for, in each delirious vision of his waking hours, her beauteous form passed like the form of Beatrice through Dante's heaven; and, as he lay in the summer afternoon, and heard at times the sound of the wind in the trees, and the sound of Sabbath bells ascending up to heaven, holy wishes and prayers ascended with them from his inmost soul, beseeching that he might not love in vain! And whenever, in silence and alone, he looked into the silent, lonely countenance of Night, he recalled the impassioned lines of Plato;—

"Lookest thou at the stars? If I were heaven,
With all the eyes of heaven would I look down on thee!"

O how beautiful it is to love! Even thou, that sneerest at this page, and laughest in cold indifference or scorn if others are near thee, thou, too, must acknowledge its truth when thou art alone; and confess, that a foolish world is prone to laugh in public, at what in private it reverences, as one of the highest impulses of our nature,—namely, Love!

One by one the objects of our affection depart from us. But our affections remain, and like vines stretch forth their broken, wounded tendrils for support. The bleeding heart needs a balm to heal it; and there is none but the love of its kind,—none but the affection of a human heart! Thus the wounded, broken affections of Flemming began to lift themselves from the dust and cling around this new object. Days and weeks passed; and, like the Student Crisostomo, he ceased to love because he began to adore. And with this adoration mingled the prayer, that, in that hour when the world is still, and the voices that praise are mute, and reflection cometh like twilight, and the maiden, in her day-dreams, counted the number of her friends, some voice in the sacred silence of her thoughts might whisper his name! And was it indeed so? Did any voice in the sacred silence of her thoughts whisper his name?—We shall soon learn.

They were sitting together one morning, on the green, flowery meadow, under the ruins of Burg Unspunnen. She was sketching the ruins. The birds were singing one and all, as if there were no aching hearts, no sin nor sorrow, in the world. So motionless was the bright air, that the shadow of the trees lay engraven on the grass. The distant snow-peaks sparkled in the sun, and nothing frowned, save the square tower of the old ruin above them.

"What a pity it is," said the lady, as she stopped to rest her weary fingers; "what a pity it is, that there is no old tradition connected with this ruin."

"I will make you one, if you wish," said Flemming.

"Can you make old traditions?"

"O yes; I made three the other day for the Rhine, and one very old one for the Black Forest. A lady with dishevelled hair; a robber with a horrible slouched hat; and a night-storm among the roaring pines."

"Delightful! Do make one for me."

"With the greatest pleasure. Where will you have the scene? Here, or in the Black Forest?"

"In the Black Forest, by all means? Begin."

"First promise not to interrupt me. If you snap the golden threads of thought, they will float away on the air like gossamer threads, and I shall never be able to recover them."

"I promise."

"Listen, then, to the Tradition of 'The Fountain of Oblivion.' "

"Begin."

Flemming was reclining on the flowery turf, at the lady's feet, looking up with dreamy eyes into her sweet face, and then into the leaves of the linden-trees overhead.

"Gentle Lady! Dost thou remember the linden-trees of Bülach, those tall and stately trees, with velvet down upon their shining leaves and rustic benches underneath their overhanging eaves! A leafy dwelling, fit to be the home of elf or fairy, where first I told my love to thee, thou cold and stately Hermione! A little peasant girl stood near, and listened all the while, with eyes of wonder and delight, and an unconscious smile, to hear the stranger still speak on in accents deep yet mild,—none else was with us in that hour, save God and that peasant child!"

"Why, it is in rhyme!"

"No, no! the rhyme is only in your imagination. You promised not to interrupt me, and you have already snapped asunder the gossamer threads of as sweet a dream as was ever spun from a poet's brain."

"It certainly did rhyme!"

"This was the reverie of the Student Hieronymus, as he sat at midnight in his chamber, with his hands clasped together, and resting upon an open volume, which he should have been reading. His pale face was raised, and the pupils of his eyes dilated as if the spirit-world were open before him, and some beauteous vision were standing there, and drawing the student's soul through his eyes up into Heaven, as the evening sun through parting summer-clouds, seems to draw into its bosom the vapors of the earth. O, it was a sweet vision! I can see it before me now!

"Near the student stood an antique bronze lamp, with strange figures carved upon it. It was a magic lamp, which once belonged to the Arabian astrologer El Geber, in Spain. Its light was beautiful as the light of stars; and, night after night, as the lonely wight sat alone and read in his lofty tower, through the

mist, and mirk, and dropping rain, it streamed out into the darkness, and was seen by many wakeful eyes. To the poor Student Hieronymus it was a wonderful Aladdin's Lamp; for in its flame a Divinity revealed herself unto him, and showed him treasures. Whenever he opened a ponderous, antiquated tome, it seemed as if some angel opened for him the gates of Paradise; and already he was known in the city as Hieronymus the Learned.

"But, alas! he could read no more. The charm was broken. Hour after hour he passed with his hands clasped before him, and his fair eyes gazing at vacancy. What could so disturb the studies of this melancholy wight? Lady, he was in love! Have you ever been in love? He had seen the face of the beautiful Hermione; and as, when we have thoughtlessly looked at the sun, our dazzled eyes, though closed, behold it still; so he beheld by day and by night the radiant image of her upon whom he had too rashly gazed. Alas! he was unhappy; for the proud Hermione disdained the love of a poor student, whose only wealth was a magic lamp. In marble halls, and amid the gay crowd that worshipped her, she had almost forgotten that such a being lived as the Student Hieronymus. The adoration of his heart had been to her only as the perfume of a wild flower, which she had carelessly crushed with her foot in passing. But he had lost all; for he had lost the quiet of his thoughts; and his agitated soul reflected only broken and distorted images of things. The world laughed at the poor student, who, in his torn and threadbare cassock, dared to lift his eyes to the Lady Hermione; while he sat alone, in his desolate chamber, and suffered in silence. He remembered many things, which he would fain forget; but which, if he had forgotten them, he would wish again to remember. Such were the linden-trees of Bülach, under whose pleasant shade he had told his love to Hermione. This was the scene which he wished most to forget, yet loved most to remember; and of this he was now dreaming, with his hands clasped upon his book, and that kind of music in his thoughts, which you, Lady, mistook for rhyme.

"Suddenly the cathedral clock struck twelve with a melancholy clang. It roused the Student Hieronymus from his dream; and rang in his ears, like the iron hoofs of the steeds of Time. The magic hour had come, when the Divinity of the lamp most willingly revealed herself to her votary. The bronze figures seemed alive; a white cloud rose from the flame and spread itself through the chamber, whose four walls dilated into magnificent cloud vistas; a fragrance, as of wild-flowers, filled the air; and a dreamy music, like distant, sweet chiming bells, announced the approach of the midnight Divinity. Through his streaming tears the heart-broken Student beheld her once more descending a pass in the snowy cloud-mountains, as, at evening, the dewy Hesperus comes from the bosom of the mist, and assumes his station in the sky. At her approach, his spirit grew more calm; for her presence was, to his feverish heart, like a tropical night,—beautiful and soothing and invigorating. At length she stood before him revealed in all her beauty; and he comprehended the visible language of her sweet but silent lips; which seemed to say;—'What would the Student Hieronymus to-night?'—'Peace!' he answered, raising his clasped hands, and smiling through his tears. 'The Student Hieronymus imploreth peace!' 'Then go,' said the spirit, 'go to the Fountain of Oblivion in the deepest solitude of the Black Forest, and cast this scroll into its waters; and thou shalt be at peace once more. Hieronymus opened his arms to embrace the Divinity, for her countenance assumed the features of Hermione; but she vanished away; the music ceased; the gorgeous cloud-land sank and fell asunder; and the student was alone within the four bare walls of his chamber. As he bowed his head downward, his eye fell upon a parchment scroll, which was lying beside the lamp. Upon it was written only the name of Hermione!

"The next morning Hieronymus put the scroll into his bosom, and went his way in search of the Fountain of Oblivion. A few days brought him to the skirts of the Black Forest. He entered, not without a feeling of dread, that land of shadows; and passed onward under melancholy pines and cedars, whose branches grew abroad and mingled together, and, as they swayed up and down, filled the air with solemn twilight

and a sound of sorrow. As he advanced into the forest, the waving moss hung, like curtains, from the branches overhead, and more and more shut out the light of heaven; and he knew that the Fountain of Oblivion was not far off. Even then the sound of falling waters was mingling with the roar of the pines overhead; and ere long he came to a river, moving in solemn majesty through the forest, and falling with a dull, leaden sound into a motionless and stagnant lake, above which the branches of the forest met and mingled, forming perpetual night. This was the Fountain of Oblivion.

"Upon its brink the student paused, and gazed into the dark waters with a steadfast look. They were limpid waters, dark with shadows only. And as he gazed, he beheld, far down in their silent depths, dim and ill-defined outlines, wavering to and fro, like the folds of a white garment in the twilight. Then more distinct and permanent shapes arose;—shapes familiar to his mind, yet forgotten and remembered again, as the fragments of a dream; till at length, far, far below him he beheld the great city of the Past, with silent marble streets, and moss-grown walls, and spires uprising with a wave-like, flickering motion. And amid the crowd that thronged those streets, he beheld faces once familiar and dear to him; and heard sorrowful, sweet voices, singing; 'O forget us not! forget us not!' and then the distant, mournful sound of funeral bells, that were tolling below, in the city of the Past. But in the gardens of that city, there were children playing, and among them, one who wore his features, as they had been in childhood. He was leading a little girl by the hand, and caressed her often, and adorned her with flowers. Then, like a dream, the scene changed, and the boy had grown older, and stood alone, gazing into the sky; and, as he gazed, his countenance changed again, and Hieronymus beheld him, as if it had been his own image in the clear water; and before him stood a beauteous maiden, whose face was like the face of Hermione, and he feared lest the scroll had fallen into the water, as he bent over it. Starting as from a dream he put his hand into his bosom and breathed freely again, when he found the scroll still there. He drew it forth, and read the blessed name of Hermione, and the city beneath him vanished away, and the air grew fragrant as with the breath of May-flowers, and a light streamed through the shadowy forest and gleamed upon the lake; and the Student Hieronymus pressed the dear name to his lips and exclaimed with streaming eyes; 'O, scorn me as thou wilt, still, still will I love thee; and thy name shall irradiate the gloom of my life, and make the waters of Oblivion smile!' And the name was no longer Hermione, but was changed to Mary; and the Student Hieronymus—is lying at your feet! O, gentle Lady!

'I did hear you talk
Far above singing; after you were gone
I grew acquainted with my heart, and searched
What stirred it so! Alas! I found it love."

CHAPTER IX

A TALK ON THE STAIRS

No! I will not describe that scene; nor how pale the stately lady sat on the border of the green, sunny meadow! The hearts of some women tremble like leaves at every breath of love which reaches them, and then are still again. Others, like the ocean, are moved only by the breath of a storm, and not so easily lulled to rest. And such was the proud heart of Mary Ashburton. It had remained unmoved by the presence of this stranger; and the sound of his footsteps and his voice excited in it no emotion. He had deceived himself! Silently they walked homeward through the green meadow. The very sunshine was sad; and the rising wind, through the old ruin above them, sounded in his ears like a hollow laugh!

Flemming went straight to his chamber. On the way, he passed the walnut trees under which he had first seen the face of Mary Ashburton. Involuntarily he closed his eyes. They were full of tears. O, there are places in this fair world, which we never wish to see again, however dear they may be to us! The towers of the old Franciscan convent never looked so gloomily as then, though the bright summer sun was shining full upon them.

In his chamber he found Berkley. He was looking out of the window, whistling.

"This evening I leave Interlachen forever," said Flemming, rather abruptly. Berkley stared.

"Indeed! Pray what is the matter? You look as pale as a ghost!"

"And have good reason to look pale," replied Flemming bitterly. "Hoffmann says, in one of his note-books, that, on the eleventh of March, at half past eight o'clock, precisely, he was an ass. That is what I was this morning at half past ten o'clock, precisely, and am now, and I suppose always shall be."

He tried to laugh, but could not. He then related to Berkley the whole story, from beginning to end.

"This is a miserable piece of business!" exclaimed Berkley, when he had finished. "Strange enough! And yet I have long ceased to marvel at the caprices of women. Did not Pan captivate the chaste Diana? Did not Titania love Nick Bottom, with his ass's head? Do you think that maidens' eyes are no longer touched with the juice of love-in-idleness! Take my word for it, she is in love with somebody else. There must be some reason for this. No; women never have any reasons, except their will. But never mind. Keep a stout heart. Care killed a cat. After all,—what is she? Who is she? Only a—"

"Hush! hush," exclaimed Flemming, in great excitement. "Not one word more, I beseech you. Do not think to console me, by depreciating her. She is very dear to me still; a beautiful, high-minded, noble woman."

"Yes," answered Berkley; "that is the way with you all, you young men. You see a sweet face, or a something, you know not what, and flickering reason says, Good night; amen to common sense. The imagination invests the beloved object with a thousand superlative charms; furnishes her with all the purple and fine linen, all the rich apparel and furniture, of human nature. I did the same when I was young. I was once as desperately in love as you are now; and went through all the

'Delicious deaths, soft exhalations
Of soul; dear and divine annihilations,
A thousand unknown rites
Of joys, and rarified delights.'

I adored and was rejected. 'You are in love with certain attributes,' said the lady. 'Damn your attributes, Madam,' said I; 'I know nothing of attributes.' 'Sir,' said she, with dignity, 'you have been drinking.' So we parted. She was married afterwards to another, who knew something about attributes, I suppose. I have seen her once since, and only once. She had a baby in a yellow gown. I hate a baby in a yellow gown. How glad I am she did not marry me. One of these days, you will be glad you have been rejected. Take my word for it."

"All that does not prevent my lot from being a very melancholy one!" said Flemming sadly.

"O, never mind the lot," cried Berkley laughing, "so long as you don't get Lot's wife. If the cucumber is bitter, throw it away, as the philosopher Marcus Antoninus says, in his Meditations. Forget her, and all will be as if you had not known her."

"I shall never forget her," replied Flemming, rather solemnly. "Not my pride, but my affections, are wounded; and the wound is too deep ever to heal. I shall carry it with me always. I enter no more into the world, but will dwell only in the world of my own thoughts. All great and unusual occurrences, whether of joy or sorrow, lift us above this earth; and we should do well always to preserve this elevation. Hitherto I have not done so. But now I will no more descend; I will sit apart and above the world, with my mournful, yet holy thoughts."

"Whew! You had better go into society; the whirl and delirium will cure you in a week. If you find a lady, who pleases you very much, and you wish to marry her, and she will not listen to such a horrid thing, I see but one remedy, which is to find another, who pleases you more, and who will listen to it."

"No, my friend; you do not understand my character," said Flemming, shaking his head. "I love this woman with a deep, and lasting affection. I shall never cease to love her. This may be madness in me; but so it is. Alas and alas! Paracelsus of old wasted life in trying to discover its elixir, which after all turned out to be alcohol; and instead of being made immortal upon earth, he died drunk on the floor of a tavern. The like happens to many of us. We waste our best years in distilling the sweetest flowers of life into love-potions, which after all do not immortalize, but only intoxicate us. By Heaven! we are all of us mad."

"But are you sure the case is utterly hopeless?"

"Utterly! utterly!"

"And yet I perceive you have not laid aside all hope. You still flatter yourself, that the lady's heart may change. The great secret of happiness consists not in enjoying, but in renouncing. But it is hard, very hard. Hope has as many lives as a cat or a king. I dare say you have heard the old Italian proverb, 'The King never dies.' But perhaps you have never heard, that, at the court of Naples, where the dead body of a monarch lies in state, his dinner is carried up to him as usual, and the court physician tastes it, to see that it be not poisoned, and then the servants bear it out again, saying 'The King does not dine to-day.' Hope in our souls is King; and we also say, 'The King never dies.' Even when in reality he lies dead within us, in a kind of solemn mockery we offer him his accustomed food, but are constrained to say, 'The King does not dine to-day.' It must be an evil day, indeed, when a king of Naples has no heart for his dinner! but you yourself are a proof, that the King never dies. You are feeding your King, although you say he is dead."

"To show you, that I do not wish to cherish hope," replied Flemming, I shall leave Interlachen to-morrow morning. I am going to the Tyrol."

"You are right," said Berkley; "there is nothing so good for sorrow as rapid motion in the open air. I shall go with you; though probably your conversation will not be very various; nothing but Edward and Kunigunde."

"What do you mean by that?"

"Go to Berlin, and you will find out. However, jesting apart, I will do all I can to cheer you, and make you forget the Dark Ladie, and this untoward accident."

"Accident!" said Flemming. "This is no accident, but God's Providence, which brought us together, to punish me for my sins."

"O, my friend," interrupted Berkley, "if you see the finger of Providence so distinctly in every act of your life, you will end by thinking yourself an Apostle and Envoy Extraordinary. I see nothing so very uncommon in what has happened to you."

"What! not when our souls are so akin to each other! When we seemed so formed to be together,—to be one!"

"I have often observed," replied Berkley coldly, "that those who are of kindred souls, rarely wed together; almost as rarely as those who are akin by blood. There seems, indeed, to be such a thing as spiritual incest. Therefore, mad lover, do not think to persuade thyself and thy scornful lady, that you have kindred souls; but rather the contrary; that you are much unlike; and each wanting in those qualities which most mark and distinguish the other. Trust me, thy courtship will then be more prosperous. But good morning. I must prepare for this sudden journey."

On the following morning, Flemming and Berkley started on their way to Innsbruck, like Huon of Bordeaux and Scherasmin on their way to Babylon. Berkley's self-assumed duty was to console his companion; a duty which he performed like an old Spanish Matadora, a woman whose business was to attend the sick, and put her elbow into the stomach of the dying to shorten their agony.

BOOK IV

Epigraph

"Mortal, they softly say,
Peace to thy heart!
We too, yes, mortal,
Have been as thou art;
Hope-lifted, doubt-depressed,
Seeing in part,
Tried, troubled, tempted,—
Sustained,—as thou art."

CHAPTER I

A MISERERE

In the Orlando Innamorato, Malagigi, the necromancer, puts all the company to sleep by reading to them from a book. Some books have this power of themselves and need no necromancer. Fearing, gentle reader, that mine may be of this kind, I have provided these introductory chapters, from time to time, like stalls or Misereres in a church, with flowery canopies and poppy-heads over them, where thou mayest sit down and sleep.

No,—the figure is not a bad one. This book does somewhat resemble a minster, in the Romanesque style, with pinnacles, and flying buttresses, and roofs,

"Gargoyled with greyhounds, and with many lions
Made of fine gold, with divers sundry dragons."

You step into its shade and coolness out of the hot streets of life; a mysterious light streams through the painted glass of the marigold windows, staining the cusps and crumpled leaves of the window-shafts, and the cherubs and holy-water-stoups below. Here and there is an image of the Virgin Mary; and other images, "in divers vestures, called weepers, stand in housings made about the tomb"; and, above all, swells the vast dome of heaven, with its star-mouldings, and the flaming constellations, like the mosaics in the dome of St. Peter's. Have you not heard funeral psalms from the chauntry? Have you not heard the sound of church-bells, as I promised; mysterious sounds from the Past and Future, as from the belfries outside the cathedral; even such a mournful, mellow, watery peal of bells, as is heard sometimes at sea, from cities afar off below the horizon?

I know not how this Romanesque, and at times flamboyant, style of architecture may please the critics. They may wish, perhaps, that I had omitted some of my many ornaments, my arabesques, and roses, and fantastic spouts, and Holy-Roods and Gallilee-steeples. But would it then have been Romanesque?

But perhaps, gentle reader, thou art one of those, who think the days of Romance gone forever. Believe it not! O, believe it not! Thou hast at this moment in thy heart as sweet a romance as was ever written. Thou art not less a woman, because thou dost not sit aloft in a tower, with a tassel-gentle on thy wrist! Thou art not less a man, because thou wearest no hauberk, nor mail-sark, and goest not on horseback after foolish adventures! Nay, nay! Every one has a Romance in his own heart. All that has blessed or awed the world lies there; and

"The oracle within him, that which lives,
He must invoke and question,—not dead books,
Not ordinances, not mould-rotten papers."

Sooner or later some passages of every one's romance must be written, either in words or actions. They will proclaim the truth; for Truth is thought, which has assumed its appropriate garments, either of words or actions; while Falsehood is thought, which, disguised in words or actions not its own, comes before the blind old world, as Jacob came before the patriarch Isaac, clothed in the goodly raiment of his brother Esau. And the world, like the patriarch, is often deceived; for, though the voice is Jacob's voice, yet the hands are the hands of Esau, and the False takes away the birth-right and the blessing from the True. Hence it is, that the world so often lifts up its voice and weeps.

That very pleasing and fanciful Chinese Romance, the Shadow in the Water, ends with the hero's marrying both the heroines. I hope my gentle reader feels curious to know the end of this Romance, which is a shadow upon the earth; and see whether there be any marriage at all in it.

That is the very point I am now thinking of, as I sit here at my pleasant chamber window, and enjoy the balmy air of a bright summer morning, and watch the motions of the golden robin, that sits on its swinging nest on the outermost, pendulous branch of yonder elm. The broad meadows and the steel-blue river remind me of the meadows of Unterseen, and the river Aar; and beyond them rise magnificent snow-white clouds, piled up like Alps. Thus the shades of Washington and William Tell seem to walk together on these Elysian Fields; for it was here, that in days long gone, our great Patriot dwelt; and yonder clouds so much resemble the snowy Alps, that they remind me irresistibly of the Swiss. Noble examples of a high purpose and a fixed will! Do they not move, Hyperion-like on high? Were they not, likewise, sons of Heaven and Earth?

Nothing can be more lovely than these summer mornings; nor than the southern window at which I sit and write, in this old mansion, which is like an Italian Villa. But O, this lassitude,—this weariness,—when all around me is so bright! I have this morning a singular longing for flowers; a wish to stroll among the roses and carnations, and inhale their breath, as if it would revive me. I wish I knew the man, who called flowers "the fugitive poetry of Nature." From this distance, from these scholastic shades,—from this leafy, blossoming, and beautiful Cambridge, I stretch forth my hand to grasp his, as the hand of a poet!—Yes; this morning I would rather stroll with him among the gay flowers, than sit here and write. I feel so weary!

Old men with their staves, says the Spanish poet, are ever knocking at the door of the grave. But I am not old. The Spanish poet might have included the young also.—No matter! Courage, and forward! The Romance must be finished; and finished soon.

O thou poor authorling! Reach a little deeper into the human heart! Touch those strings,—touch those deeper strings, and more boldly, or the notes will die away like whispers, and no ear shall hear them, save thine own! And, to cheer thy solitary labor, remember, that the secret studies of an author are the sunken piers upon which is to rest the bridge of his fame, spanning the dark waters of Oblivion. They are out of sight; but without them no superstructure can stand secure!

And now, Reader, since the sermon is over, and we are still sitting here in this Miserere, let us read aloud a page from the old parchment manuscript on the lettern before us; let us sing it through these dusky aisles, like a Gregorian Chant, and startle the sleeping congregation!

"I have read of the great river Euripus, which ebbeth and floweth seven times a day, and with such violence, that it carrieth ships upon it with full sail, directly against the wind. Seven times in an hour ebbeth and floweth rash opinion, in the torrent of indiscreet and troublesome apprehensions; carrying critic calumny and squint-eyed detraction mainly against the wind of wisdom and judgment."

In secula seculorum! Amen!

CHAPTER II

CURFEW BELLS

Welcome Disappointment! Thy hand is cold and hard, but it is the hand of a friend! Thy voice is stern and harsh, but it is the voice of a friend! O, there is something sublime in calm endurance, something sublime in the resolute, fixed purpose of suffering without complaining, which makes disappointment oftentimes better than success!

The emperor Isaac Angelus made a treaty with Saladin, and tried to purchase the Holy Sepulchre with gold. Richard Lion-heart scorned such alliance, and sought to recover it by battle. Thus do weak minds make treaties with the passions they cannot overcome, and try to purchase happiness at the expense of principle. But the resolute will of a strong man scorns such means; and struggles nobly with his foe, to achieve great deeds. Therefore, whosoever thou art that sufferest, try not to dissipate thy sorrow by the breath of the world, nor drown its voice in thoughtless merriment. It is a treacherous peace that is purchased by indulgence. Rather take this sorrow to thy heart, and make it a part of thee, and it shall nourish thee till thou art strong again.

The shadows of the mind are like those of the body. In the morning of life they all lie behind us; at noon, we trample them under foot; and in the evening they stretch long, broad, and deepening before us. Are not, then, the sorrows of childhood as dark as those of age? Are not the morning shadows of life as deep and broad as those of its evening? Yes; but morning shadows soon fade away, while those of evening reach forward into the night and mingle with the coming darkness. Man is begotten in delight and born in pain; and in these are the rapture and labor of his life fore-shadowed from the beginning. But the life of man upon this fair earth is made up for the most part of little pains and little pleasures. The great wonder-flowers bloom but once in a lifetime.

A week had already elapsed since the events recorded in the last chapter. Paul Flemming went his way, a melancholy man, "drinking the sweet wormwood of his sorrow." He did not rail at Providence and call it fate, but suffered and was silent. It is a beautiful trait in the lover's character, that he thinks no evil of the object loved. What he suffered was no swift storm of feeling, that passes away with a noise, and leaves the heart clearer; but a dark phantom had risen up in the clear night, and, like that of Adamastor, hid the stars; and if it ever vanished away for a season, still the deep sound of the moaning main would be heard afar, through many a dark and lonely hour. And thus he journeyed on, wrapped in desponding gloom, and mainly heedless of all things around him. His mind was distempered. That one face was always before him; that one voice forever saying;

"You are not the Magician."

Painful, indeed, it is to be misunderstood and undervalued by those we love. But this, too, in our life, must we learn to bear without a murmur; for it is a tale often repeated.

There are persons in this world to whom all local associations are naught. The genius of the place speaks not to them. Even on battle-fields, where the voice of this genius is wont to be loudest, they hear only the sound of their own voices; they meet there only their own dull and pedantic thoughts, as the old grammarian Brunetto Latini met on the plain of Roncesvalles a poor student riding on a bay mule. This was not always the case with Paul Flemming, but it had become so now. He felt no interest in the scenery around him. He hardly looked at it. Even the difficult mountain-passes, where, from his rocky eyrie the eagle-eyed Tyrolese peasant had watched his foe, and the roaring, turbid torrent underneath, which had swallowed up the bloody corse, that fell from the rocks like a crushed worm, awakened no

lively emotion in his breast. All around him seemed dreamy and vague; all within dim, as in a sun's eclipse. As the moon, whether visible or invisible, has power over the tides of the ocean, so the face of that lady, whether present or absent, had power over the tides of his soul; both by day and night, both waking and sleeping. In every pale face and dark eye he saw a resemblance to her; and what the day denied him in reality, the night gave him in dreams.

"This is a strange, fantastic world," said Berkley, after a very long silence, during which the two travellers had been sitting each in his corner of the travelling carriage, wrapped in his own reflections. "A very strange, fantastic world; where each one pursues his own golden bubble, and laughs at his neighbour for doing the same. I have been thinking how a moral Linnæus would classify our race. I think he would divide it, not as Lord Byron did, into two great classes, the bores and those who are bored, but into three, namely; Happy Men, Lucky Dogs, and Miserable Wretches. This is more true and philosophical, though perhaps not quite so comprehensive. He is the Happy Man, who, blessed with modest ease, a wife and children,—sits enthroned in the hearts of his family, and knows no other ambition, than that of making those around him happy. But the Lucky Dog is he, who, free from all domestic cares, saunters up and down his room, in morning gown and slippers; drums on the window of a rainy day; and, as he stirs his evening fire, snaps his fingers at the world, and says, 'I have no wife nor children, good or bad, to provide for.' I had a friend, who is now no more. He was taken away in the bloom of life, by a very rapid—widow. He was by birth and by profession a beau,—born with a quizzing-glass and a cane. Cock of the walk, he flapped his wings, and crowed among the feathered tribe. But alas! a fair, white partlet has torn his crest out, and he shall crow no more. You will generally find him of a morning, smelling round a beef-cart, with domestic felicity written in every line of his countenance; and sometimes meet him in a cross-street at noon, hurrying homeward, with a beef-steak on a wooden skewer, or a fresh fish, with a piece of tarred twine run through its gills. In the evening he rocks the cradle, and gets up in the night when the child cries. Like a Goth, of the Dark Ages, he consults his wife on all mighty matters, and looks upon her as a being of more than human goodness and wisdom. In short, the ladies all say he is a very domestic man, and makes a good husband; which, under the rose, is only a more polite way of saying he is hen-pecked. He is a Happy Man. I have another dear friend, who is a sexagenary bachelor. He has one of those well-oiled dispositions, which turn upon the hinges of the world without creaking. The hey-day of life is over with him; but his old age is sunny and chirping; and a merry heart still nestles in his tottering frame, like a swallow that builds in a tumble-down chimney. He is a professed Squire of Dames. The rustle of a silk gown is music to his ears, and his imagination is continually lantern-led by some will-with-a-wisp in the shape of a lady's stomacher. In his devotion to the fair sex,—the muslin, as he calls it,—he is the gentle flower of chivalry. It is amusing to see how quick he strikes into the scent of a lady's handkerchief. When once fairly in pursuit, there is no such thing as throwing him out. His heart looks out at his eye; and his inward delight tingles down to the tail of his coat. He loves to bask in the sunshine of a smile; when he can breathe the sweet atmosphere of kid gloves and cambric handkerchiefs, his soul is in its element; and his supreme delight is to pass the morning, to use his own quaint language, 'in making dodging calls, and wiggling round among the ladies!' He is a lucky dog!"

"And as a specimen of the class of Miserable Wretches, I suppose you will take me," said Flemming, making an effort to enter into his friend's humor. "Certainly I am wretched enough. You may make me the stuffed bear,—the specimen of this class."

"By no means," replied Berkley; "you are not reduced so low. He only is utterly wretched, who is the slave of his own passions, or those of others. This, I trust, will never be your condition. Why so wan and pale, fond lover? Do you remember Sir John Suckling's Song?

'Why so wan and pale, fond lover;
Pr'ythee why so pale?
Will, if looking well can't move her,
Looking ill prevail?
Pr'ythee why so pale?

'Why so dull and mute, young sinner;
Pr'ythee why so mute?
Will, if speaking well can't win her,
Saying nothing do 't?
Pr'ythee why so mute?

'Quit, quit, for shame! this cannot move,
This cannot take her!
If of herself she do not love,
Nothing will make her!
The devil take her!'
How do you like that?"

"To you I say quit, quit for shame;" replied Flemming. "Why quote the songs of that witty and licentious age? Have you no better consolation to offer me? How many, many times must I tell you, that I bear the lady no ill-will. I do not blame her for not loving me. I desire her happiness, even at the sacrifice of my own."

"That is generous in you, and deserves a better fate. But you are so figurative in all you say, that a stranger would think you had no real feeling,—and only fancied yourself in love."

"Expression of feeling is different with different minds. It is not always simple. Some minds, when excited, naturally speak in figures and similitudes. They do not on that account feel less deeply. This is obvious in our commonest modes of speech. It depends upon the individual."

"Kyrie Eleëson!"

"Well, abuse my figures of speech as much as you please. What I insist upon is, that you shall not abuse the lady. When did you ever hear me breathe a whisper against her?"

"Oho! Now you speak like Launce to his dog!"

Their conversation, which had begun so merrily, was here suddenly interrupted by a rattling peal of thunder, that announced a near-approaching storm. It was late in the afternoon, and the whole heaven black with low, trailing clouds. Still blacker the storm came sailing up majestically from the southwest, with almost unbroken volleys of distant thunder. The wind seemed to be storming a cloud redoubt; and marched onward with dust, and the green banners of the trees flapping in the air, and heavy cannonading, and occasionally an explosion, like the blowing up of a powder-wagon. Mingled with this was the sound of thunder-bells from a village not far off. They were all ringing dolefully to ward off the thunderbolt. At the entrance of the village stood a large wooden crucifix; around which was a crowd of priests and peasants, kneeling in the wet grass, by the roadside, with their hands and eyes lifted to heaven, and praying for rain. Their prayer was soon answered.

The travellers drove on with the driving wind and rain. They had come from Landeck, and hoped to reach Innsbruck before midnight. Night closed in, and Flemming fell asleep with the loud storm overhead, and at his feet the roaring Inn, a mountain torrent leaping onward as wild and restless, as when it first sprang from its cradle in the solitudes of Engaddin; meet emblem of himself, thus rushing through the night. His slumber was long, but broken; and at length he awoke in terror; for he heard a voice pronounce in his ear distinctly these words;

"They have brought the dead body."

They were driving by a churchyard at the entrance of a town; and among the tombs a dim lamp was burning before an image of the Virgin. It had a most unearthly appearance. Flemming almost feared to see the congregation of the dead go into the church and sing their midnight mass. He spoke to Berkley; but received no answer; he was in a deep sleep.

"Then it was only a dream," said he to himself; "yet how distinct the voice was! O, if we had spiritual organs, to see and hear things now invisible and inaudible to us, we should behold the whole air filled with the departing souls of that vast multitude which every moment dies,—should behold them streaming up like thin vapors heaven-ward, and hear the startling blast of the archangel's trump sounding incessant through the universe and proclaiming the awful judgment day. Truly the soul departs not alone on its last journey, but spirits of its kind attend it, when not ministering angels; and they go in families to the unknown land! Neither in life nor in death are we alone."

He slept again at intervals; and at length, though long after midnight, reached Innsbruck between sleeping and waking; his mind filled with dim recollections of the unspeakably dismal night-journey;— the climbing of hills, and plunging into dark ravines;—the momentary rattling of the wheels over paved streets of towns, and the succeeding hollow rolling and tramping on the wet earth;—the blackness of the night;—the thunder and lightning and rain; the roar of waters, leaping through deep chasms by the road-side, and the wind through the mountain-passes, sounding loud and long, like the irrepressible laughter of the gods.

The travellers on the morrow lingered not long in Innsbruck. They did not fail, however, to visit the tomb of Maximilian in the Franciscan Church of the Holy Cross, and gaze with some admiration upon the twenty-eight gigantic bronze statues of Godfrey of Bouillon, and King Arthur and Ernest the Iron-man, and Frederick of the Empty Pockets, kings and heroes, and others, which stand leaning on their swords between the columns of the church, as if guarding the tomb of the dead. These statues reminded Flemming of the bronze giants, which strike the hours on the belfry of San Basso, in Venice, and of the flail-armed monsters, that guarded the gateway of Angulaffer's castle in Oberon. After gazing awhile at these motionless sentinels, they went forth, and strolled through the public gardens, with the jagged mountains right over their heads, and all around them tall, melancholy pines, like Tyrolese peasants, with shaggy hair; and at their feet the mad torrent of the Inn, sweeping with turbid waves through the midst of the town. In the afternoon they drove on towards Salzburg through the magnificent mountain-passes of Waidering and Unken.

CHAPTER III

On the following morning Flemming awoke in a chamber of the Golden Ship at Salzburg, just as the clock in the Dome-church opposite was striking ten. The window-shutters were closed, and the room nearly dark. He was lying on his back, with his hands crossed upon his breast, and his eyes looking up at the white curtains overhead. He thought them the white marble canopy of a tomb, and himself the marble statue, lying beneath. When the clock ceased striking, the eight and twenty gigantic bronze statues from the Church of Holy Rood in Innsbruck stalked into the chamber, and arranged themselves along the walls, which spread into dimly-lighted aisles and arches. On the painted windows he saw Interlachen, with its Franciscan cloister, and the Square Tower of the ruins. In a pendent, overhead, stood the German student, as Saint Vitus; and on a lavatory, or basin of holy-water, below, sat a cherub, with the form and features of Berkley. Then the organ-pipes began to blow, and he heard the voices of an invisible choir chanting. And anon the gilded gates in the bronze screen before the chancel opened, and a bridal procession passed through. The bride was clothed in the garb of the Middle Ages; and held a book in her hand, with velvet covers, and golden clasps. It was Mary Ashburton. She looked at him as she passed. Her face was pale; and there were tears in her sweet eyes. Then the gates closed again; and one of the oaken poppy-heads over a carved stall, in the shape of an owl, flapped its broad wings, and hooted, "Towhit! to-whoo!" Then the whole scene changed; and he thought himself a monk's-head on a gutterspout; and it rained dismally; and Berkley was standing under with an umbrella, laughing!

In other words, Flemming was in a raging fever, and delirious. He remained in this state for a week. The first thing he was conscious of was hearing the doctor say to Berkley;

"The crisis is passed. I now consider him out of danger."

He then fell into a sweet sleep; the wild fever had swept away like an angry, red cloud, and the refreshing summer rain began to fall like dew upon the parched earth. Still another week; and Flemming was, "sitting clothed, and in his right mind." Berkley had been reading to him; and still held the book in his hand, with his fore-finger between the leaves. It was a volume of Hoffmann's writings.

"How very strange it is," said he, "that you can hardly open the biography of any German author, but you will find it begin with an account of his grandfather. It will tell you how the venerable old man walked up and down the garden among the gay flowers, wrapped in his morning gown, which is likewise covered with flowers, and perhaps wearing on his head a little velvet cap. Or you will find him sitting by the chimney-corner in the great chair, smoking his ancestral pipe, with shaggy eyebrows and eyes like birds nests under the eaves of a house, and a mouth like a Nuremberg nutcracker's. The future poet climbs upon the old man's knees. His genius is not recognised yet. He is thought for the most part a dull boy. His father is an austere man, or perhaps dead. But the mother is still there, a sickly, saint-like woman, with knitting-work, and an elder sister, who has already been in love, and wears rings on her fingers;—

'Death's heads, and such mementos,
Her grandmother and worm-eaten aunts left to her,
To tell her what her beauty must arrive at.'"

"But this is not the case with the life of Hoffmann, if I recollect right."

"No, not precisely. Instead of the grandfather we have the grandmother, a stately dame, who has long since shaken hands with the vanities of life. The mother, separated from her husband, is sick in mind and body, and flits to and fro, like a shadow. Then there is an affectionate maiden aunt; and an uncle, a retired judge, the terror of little boys,—the Giant Despair of this Doubting Castle in Koenigsberg; and occasionally the benign countenance of a venerable grand-uncle, whom Lamotte Fouqué called a hero of the olden time in morning gown and slippers, looks in at the door and smiles. In the upper story of the same house lived a poor boy with his mother, who was so far crazed as to believe herself to be the Virgin Mary, and her son the Saviour of the world. Wild fancies, likewise, were to sweep through the brain of that child. He was to meet Hoffmann elsewhere and be his friend in after years, though as yet they knew nothing of each other. This was Werner, who has made some noise in German literature as the author of many wild Destiny-Dramas."

"Hoffmann died, I believe, in Berlin."

"Yes. He left Koenigsberg at twenty years of age, and passed the next eight years of his life in the Prussian-Polish Provinces, where he held some petty office under government; and took to himself many bad habits and a Polish wife. After this he was Music-Director at various German theatres, and led a wandering, wretched life for ten years. He then went to Berlin as Clerk of the Exchange, and there remained till his death, which took place some seven or eight years afterward."

"Did you ever see him?"

"I was in Berlin during his lifetime, and saw him frequently. I shall never forget the first time. It was at one of the æsthetic Teas, given by a literary lady Unter den Linden, where the lions were fed with convenient food, from tea and bread and butter, up to oysters and Rhine-wine. During the evening my attention was arrested by the entrance of a strange little figure, with a wild head of brown hair. His eyes were bright gray; and his thin lips closely pressed together with an expression of not unpleasing irony. This strange looking personage began to bow his way through the crowd, with quick, nervous, hinge-like motions, much resembling those of a marionette. He had a hoarse voice, and such a rapid utterance, that although I understood German well enough for ordinary purposes, I could not understand one half he said. Ere long he had seated himself at the piano-forte, and was improvising such wild, sweet fancies, that the music of one's dreams is not more sweet and wild. Then suddenly some painful thought seemed to pass over his mind, as if he imagined, that he was there to amuse the company. He rose from the piano-forte, and seated himself in another part of the room; where he began to make grimaces, and talk loud while others were singing. Finally he disappeared, like a hobgoblin, laughing, 'Ho! ho! ho!' I asked a person beside me who this strange being was. 'That was Hoffmann,' was the answer. 'The Devil!' said I. 'Yes,' continued my informant; 'and if you should follow him now, you would see him plunge into an obscure and unfrequented wine-cellar, and there, amid boon companions, with wine and tobacco-smoke, and quirks and quibbles, and quaint, witty sayings, turn the dim night into glorious day.'"

"What a strange being!"

"I once saw him at one of his night-carouses. He was sitting in his glory, at the head of the table; not stupidly drunk, but warmed with wine, which made him madly eloquent, as the Devil's Elixir did the Monk Medardus. There, in the full tide of witty discourse, or, if silent, his gray, hawk eye flashing from beneath his matted hair, and taking note of all that was grotesque in the company round him, sat this unfortunate genius, till the day began to dawn. Then he found his way homeward, having, like the souls of the envious in Purgatory, his eyelids sewed together with iron wire;—though his was from

champagne bottles. At such hours he wrote his wild, fantastic tales. To his excited fancy everything assumed a spectral look. The shadows of familiar things about him stalked like ghosts through the haunted chambers of his soul; and the old portraits on the walls winked at him, and seemed stepping down from their frames; till, aghast at the spectral throng about him, he would call his wife from her bed, to sit by him while he wrote."

"No wonder he died in the prime of life!"

"No. The only wonder is, that he could have followed this course of life for six years. I am astonished that it did not kill him sooner."

"But death came at last in an appalling shape."

"Yes; his forty-sixth birth day found him sitting at home in his arm-chair, with his friends around him. But the rare old wine,—he always drank the best,—touched not the sick-man's lips that night. His wonted humor was gone. Of all his 'jibes, his gambols, his songs, his flashes of merriment, that were wont to set the table on a roar, not one now, to mock his own grinning!—quite chap-fallen.'—The conversation was of death and the grave. And when one of his friends said, that life was not the highest good, Hoffmann interrupted him, exclaiming with a startling earnestness; 'No, no! Life, life, only life! on any condition whatsoever!' Five months after this he had ceased to suffer, because he had ceased to live. He died piecemeal. His feet and hands, his legs and arms, gradually, and in succession, became motionless, dead. But his spirit was not dead, nor motionless; and, through the solitary day or sleepless night, lying in his bed, he dictated to an amanuensis his last stories. Strange stories, indeed, were they for a dying man to write! Yet such delight did he take in dictating them, that he said to his friend Hitzig, that, upon the whole, he was willing to give up forever the use of his hands, if he could but preserve the power of writing by dictation. Such was his love of life,—of what he called the sweet habitude of being!"

"Was it not he, who in his last hours expressed such a longing to behold the green fields once more; and exclaimed; 'Heaven! it is already summer, and I have not yet seen a single green tree!'"

"Yes, that was Hoffmann. Soon afterwards he died. The closing scene was striking. He gradually lost all sensation, though his mind remained vigorous. Feeling no more pain, he said to his physician; 'It will soon be over now. I feel no more pain.' He thought himself well again; but the physician knew that he was dying, and said; 'Yes, it will soon be over!' The next morning he called his wife to his bed-side; and begged her to fold his motionless hands together. Then, as he raised his eyes to heaven, she heard him say, 'We must, then, think of God, also!' More sorrowful words than these have seldom fallen from the lips of man. Shortly afterwards the flame of life glared up within him; he said he was well again; that in the evening he should go on with the story he was writing; and wished that the last sentence might be read over to him. Shortly after this they turned his face to the wall, and he died."

"And thus passed to its account a human soul, after much self-inflicted suffering. Let us tread lightly upon the poet's ashes. For my part, I confess, that I have not the heart to take him from the general crowd of erring, sinful men, and judge him harshly. The little I have seen of the world, and know of the history of mankind, teaches me to look upon the errors of others in sorrow, not in anger. When I take the history of one poor heart that has sinned and suffered, and represent to myself the struggles and temptations it has passed,—the brief pulsations of joy,—the feverish inquie-tude of hope and fear,—the tears of regret,—the feebleness of purpose,—the pressure of want,—the desertion of friends,—the scorn of a world that has little charity,—the desolation of the soul's sanctuary,—and threatening voices

within,—health gone,—happiness gone,—even hope, that stays longest with us, gone,—I have little heart for aught else than thankfulness, that it is not so with me, and would fain leave the erring soul of my fellow-man with Him, from whose hands it came,

'even as a little child,
Weeping and laughing in its childish sport.'"

"You are right. And it is worth a student's while to observe calmly how tobacco, wine, and midnight did their work like fiends upon the delicate frame of Hoffmann; and no less thoroughly upon his delicate mind. He who drinks beer, thinks beer; and he who drinks wine, thinks wine;—and he who drinks midnight, thinks midnight. He was a man of rare intellect. He was endowed with racy humor and sarcastic wit, and a glorious imagination. But the fire of his genius burned not peacefully, and with a steady flame, upon the hearth of his home. It was a glaring and irregular flame;—for the branches that he fed it with, were not branches from the Tree of Life,—but from another tree that grew in Paradise,—and they were wet with the unhealthy dews of night, and more unhealthy wine; and thus, amid smoke and ashes the fire burned fitfully, and went out with a glare, which leaves the beholder blind."

"This fire within him was a Meleager's fire-brand; and, when it burned out, he died. And, as you say, marks of all this are clearly visible in Hoffmann's writings. Indeed, when I read his strange fancies, it is with me, as when in the summer night I hear the rising wind among the trees, and the branches bow, and beckon with their long fingers, and voices go gibbering and mocking through the air. A feeling of awe and mysterious dread comes over me. I wish to hear the sound of living voice or footstep near me,—to see a friendly and familiar face. In truth, if it be late at night, the reader as well as the writer of these unearthly fancies, would fain have a patient, meek-eyed wife, with her knitting-work, at his elbow."

Berkley smiled; but Flemming continued without noticing the smile, though he knew what was passing in the mind of his friend;

"The life and writings of this singular being interest me in a high degree. Oftentimes one may learn more from a man's errors, than from his virtues. Moreover, from the common sympathies of our nature, souls that have struggled and suffered are dear to me. Willingly do I recognise their brotherhood. Scars upon their foreheads do not so deform them, that they cease to interest. They are always signs of struggle; though alas! too often, likewise, of defeat. Seasons of unhealthy, dreamy, vague delight, are followed by seasons of weariness and darkness. Where are then the bright fancies, that, amid the great stillness of the night, arise like stars in the firmament of our souls? The morning dawns, the light of common day shines in upon us, and the heavens are without a star! From the lives of such men we learn, that mere pleasant sensations are not happiness;—that sensual pleasures are to be drunk sparingly, and, as it were, from the palm of the hand; and that those who bow down upon their knees to drink of these bright streams that water life, are not chosen of God either to overthrow or to overcome!"

"I think you are very lenient in your judgment. This is not the usual defect of critics. Like Shakspeare's samphire-gatherer, they have a dreadful trade! and, to make the simile complete, they ought to hang for it!"

"Methinks it would be hard to hang a man for the sake of a simile. But which of Hoffmann's works is it, that you have in your hand?"

"His Phatasy-Pieces in Callot's manner. Who was this Callot?"

"He was a Lorrain painter of the seventeenth century, celebrated for his wild and grotesque conceptions. These sketches of Hoffmann are imitations of his style. They are full of humor, poetry, and brilliant imagination."

"And which of them shall I read to you? The Ritter Glück; or the Musical Sufferings of John Kreisler; or that very exquisite story of the Golden Jar, wherein is depicted the life of Poesy, in this common-place world of ours?"

"Read the shortest. Read Kreisler. That will amuse me. It is a picture of his own sufferings at the æsthetic Teas in Berlin, supposed to be written in pencil on the blank leaves of a music-book."

Thereupon Berkley leaned back in his easy chair, and read as follows.

CHAPTER IV

MUSICAL

SUFFERINGS OF JOHN KREISLER.

"They are all gone! I might have known it by the whispering, shuffling, coughing, buzzing through all the notes of the gamut. It was a true swarm of bees, leaving the old hive. Gottlieb has lighted fresh candles for me, and placed a bottle of Burgundy on the piano-forte. I can play no more, I am perfectly exhausted. My glorious old friend here on the music-stand is to blame for that. Again he has borne me away through the air, as Mephistopheles did Faust, and so high, that I took not the slightest notice of the little men under me, though I dare say they made noise enough. A rascally, worthless, wasted evening! But now I am well and merry! However, while I was playing, I took out my pencil, and on page sixty-three, under the last system, noted down a couple of good flourishes in cipher with my right hand, while the left was struggling away in the torrent of sweet sounds. Upon the blank page at the end I go on writing. I leave all ciphers and sweet tones, and with true delight, like a sick man restored to health, who can never stop relating what he has suffered, I note down here circumstantially the dire agonies of this evening's tea-party. And not for myself alone, but likewise for all those who from time to time may amuse and edify themselves with my copy of John Sebastian Bach's Variations for the Piano-forte, published by Nägeli in Zürich, and who find my marks at the end of the thirtieth variation, and, led on by the great Latin Verte, (I will write it down the moment I get through this doleful statement of grievances,) turn over the leaf and read.

"They will at once see the connexion. They know, that the Geheimerath Rödelein's house is a charming house to visit in, and that he has two daughters, of whom the whole fashionable world proclaims with enthusiasm, that they dance like goddesses, speak French like angels, and play and sing and draw like the Muses. The Geheimerath Rödelein is a rich man. At his quarterly dinners he brings on the most delicious wines and richest dishes. All is established on a footing of the greatest elegance; and whoever at his tea-parties does not amuse himself heavenly, has no ton, no esprit, and particularly no taste for the fine arts. It is with an eye to these, that, with the tea, punch, wine, ice-creams, etc., a little music is

always served up, which, like the other refreshments, is very quietly swallowed by the fashionable world.

"The arrangements are as follows.—After every guest has had time enough to drink as many cups of tea as he may wish, and punch and ices have been handed round twice, the servants wheel out the card-tables for the elder and more solid part of the company, who had rather play cards than any musical instrument; and, to tell the truth, this kind of playing does not make such a useless noise as others, and you hear only the clink of money.

"This is a hint for the younger part of the company to pounce upon the Misses Rödelein. A great tumult ensues; in the midst of which you can distinguish these words,—

"'Schönes Fräulein! do not refuse us the gratification of your heavenly talent! O, sing something! that's a good dear!—impossible,—bad cold,—the last ball! have not practised anything,—oh, do, do, we beg of you,' etc.

"Meanwhile Gottlieb has opened the piano-forte, and placed the well-known music-book on the stand; and from the card-table cries the respectable mamma,—

" 'Chantez donc, mes enfans!'

"That is the cue of my part. I place myself at the piano-forte, and the Rödeleins are led up to the instrument in triumph.

"And now another difficulty arises. Neither wishes to sing first.

"'You know, dear Nanette, how dreadful hoarse I am.'

"'Why, my dear Marie, I am as hoarse as you are.'

"'I sing so badly!—'

"'O, my dear child; do begin!'

"My suggestion, (I always make the same!) that they should both begin together with a duet, is loudly applauded;—the music-book is thumbed over, and the leaf, carefully folded down, is at length found, and away we go with Dolce dell' anima, etc.

"To tell the truth, the talent of the Misses Rödelein is not the smallest. I have been an instructer here only five years, and little short of two years in the Rödelein family. In this short time, Fräulein Nanette has made such progress, that a tune, which she has heard at the theatre only ten times, and has played on the piano-forte, at farthest, ten times more, she will sing right off, so that you know in a moment what it is. Fräulein Marie catches it at the eighth time; and if she is sometimes a quarter of a note lower than the piano-forte, after all it is very tolerable, considering her pretty little doll-face, and very passable rosy-lips.

"After the duet, a universal chorus of applause! And now arriettas and duettinos succeed each other, and right merrily I hammer away at the thousand-times-repeated accompaniment. During the singing,

the Finanzräthin Eberstein, by coughing and humming, has given to understand that she also sings. Fräulein Nanette says;

"'But, my dear Finanzräthin, now you must let us hear your exquisite voice.'

"A new tumult arises. She has a bad cold in her head,—she does not know anything by heart! Gottlieb brings straightway two armfuls of music-books; and the leaves are turned over again and again. First she thinks she will sing Der Hölle Rache, etc., then Hebe sich, etc., then Ach, Ich liebte, etc. In this embarrassment, I propose, Ein Veilchen auf der Wiese, etc. But she is for the heroic style; she wants to make a display, and finally selects the aria in Constantia.

"O scream, squeak, mew, gurgle, groan, agonize, quiver, quaver, just as much as you please, Madam,—I have my foot on the fortissimo pedal, and thunder myself deaf! O Satan, Satan! which of thy goblins damned has got into this throat, pinching, and kicking, and cuffing the tones about so! Four strings have snapped already, and one hammer is lamed for life. My ears ring again,—my head hums,—my nerves tremble! Have all the harsh notes from the cracked trumpet of a strolling-player been imprisoned in this little throat! (But this excites me,—I must drink a glass of Burgundy.)

"The applause was unbounded; and some one observed, that the Finanzräthin and Mozart had put me quite in a blaze. I smiled with downcast eyes, very stupidly. I could but acknowledge it. And now all talents, which hitherto had bloomed unseen, were in motion, wildly flitting to and fro. They were bent upon a surfeit of music; tuttis, finales, choruses must be performed. The Canonicus Kratzer sings, you know, a heavenly bass, as was observed by the gentleman yonder, with the head of Titus Andronicus, who modestly remarked also, that he himself was properly only a second-ratetenor; but, though he said it, who should not say it, was nevertheless member of several academies of music. Forthwith preparations are made for the first chorus in the opera of Titus. It went off gloriously. The Canonicus, standing close behind me, thundered out the bass over my head, as if he were singing with bass-drums and trumpet obbligato in a cathedral. He struck the notes gloriously; but in his hurry he got the tempo just about twice too slow. However, he was true to himself at least in this, that through the whole piece he dragged along just half a beat behind the rest. The others showed a most decided penchant for the ancient Greek music, which, as is well known, having nothing to do with harmony, ran on in unison or monotone. They all sang treble, with slight variations, caused by accidental rising and falling of the voice, say some quarter of a note.

"This somewhat noisy affair produced a universal tragic state of feeling, namely a kind of terror, even at the card-tables, which for the moment could no longer, as before, chime in melodramatic, by weaving into the music sundry exclamations; as, for instance;

" 'O! I loved,—eight and forty,—was so happy,—I pass,—then I knew not,—whist,—pangs of love,—follow suit,' etc.—It has a very pretty effect. (I fill my glass.)

"That was the highest point of the musical exhibition this evening. 'Now it is all over,' thought I to myself. I shut the book, and got up from the piano-forte. But the baron, my ancient tenor, came up to me, and said;

" 'My dear Herr Capellmeister, they say you play the most exquisite voluntaries! Now do play us one; only a short one, I entreat you!'

"I answered very drily, that to-day my fantasies had all gone a wool-gathering; and, while we are talking about it, a devil, in the shape of a dandy, with two waistcoats, had smelt out Bach's Variations, which were lying under my hat in the next room. He thinks they are merely little variations, such as Nel cor mio non più sento, or Ah, vous dirai-je, maman, etc., and insists upon it, that I shall play them. I try to excuse myself, but they all attack me. So then, 'Listen, and burst with ennui,' think I to myself,—and begin to work away.

"When I had got to variation number three, several ladies departed, followed by the gentleman with the Titus-Andronicus head. The Rödeleins, as their teacher was playing, stood it out, though not without difficulty, to number twelve. Number fifteen made the man with two waistcoats take to his heels. Out of most excessive politeness, the Baron stayed till number thirty, and drank up all the punch, which Gottlieb placed on the piano-forte for me.

"I should have brought all to a happy conclusion, but, alas! this number thirty,—the theme,—tore me irresistibly away. Suddenly the quarto leaves spread out to a gigantic folio, on which a thousand imitations and developments of the theme stood written, and I could not choose but play them. The notes became alive, and glimmered and hopped all round about me,—an electric fire streamed through the tips of my fingers into the keys,—the spirit, from which it gushed forth, spread his broad wings over my soul, the whole room was filled with a thick mist, in which the candles burned dim,—and through which peered forth now a nose, and anon a pair of eyes, and then suddenly vanished away again. And thus it came to pass, that I was left alone with my Sebastian Bach, by Gottlieb attended, as by a familiar spirit. (Your good health, Sir.)

"Is an honest musician to be tormented with music, as I have been to-day, and am so often tormented? Verily, no art is so damnably abused, as this same glorious, holy Musica, who, in her delicate being, is so easily desecrated. Have you real talent,—real feeling for art? Then study music;—do something worthy of the art,—and dedicate your whole soul to the beloved saint. If without this you have a fancy for quavers and demi-semi-quavers, practise for yourself and by yourself, and torment not therewith the Capellmeister Kreisler and others.

"Well, now I might go home, and put the finishing touch to my sonata for the piano-forte; but it is not yet eleven o'clock, and, withal, a beautiful summer night. I will lay any wager, that, at my next-door neighbour's, (the Oberjägermeister,) the young ladies are sitting at the window, screaming down into the street, for the twentieth time, with harsh, sharp, piercing voices, 'When thine eye is beaming love,'—but only the first stanza, over and over again. Obliquely across the way, some one is murdering the flute, and has, moreover, lungs like Rameau's nephew; and, in notes of 'linked sweetness long drawn out,' his neighbour is trying acoustic experiments on the French horn. The numerous dogs of the neighbourhood are growing unquiet, and my landlord's cat, inspired by that sweet duet, is making close by my window (for, of course, my musico-poetic laboratory is an attic,) certain tender confessions,—upward through the whole chromatic scale, soft complaining, to the neighbour's puss, with whom he has been in love since March last! Till this is all fairly over, Il think will sit quietly here. Besides, there is still blank paper and Burgundy left, of which I forthwith take a sip.

"There is, as I have heard, an ancient law, forbidding those, who followed any noisy handicraft, from living near literary men. Should not then musical composers, poor, and hard beset, and who, moreover, are forced to coin their inspiration into gold, to spin out the thread of life withal, be allowed to apply this law to themselves, and banish out of the neighbourhood all ballad-singers and bagpipers? What would a painter say, while transferring to his canvass a form of ideal beauty, if you should hold up

before him all manner of wild faces and ugly masks? He might shut his eyes, and in this way, at least, quietly follow out the images of fancy. Cotton, in one's ears, is of no use; one still hears the dreadful massacre. And then the idea,—the bare idea, 'Now they are going to sing,—now the horn strikes up,'—is enough to send one's sublimest conceptions to the very devil."

CHAPTER V

SAINT GILGEN

It was a bright Sunday morning when Flemming and Berkley left behind them the cloud-capped hills of Salzburg, and journeyed eastward towards the lakes. The landscape around them was one to attune their souls to holy musings. Field, forest, hill and vale, fresh air, and the perfume of clover-fields and new-mown hay, birds singing, and the sound of village bells, and the moving breeze among the branches,—no laborers in the fields, but peasants on their way to church, coming across the green pastures, with roses in their hats,—the beauty and quiet of the holy day of rest,—all, all in earth and air, breathed upon the soul like a benediction.

They stopped to change horses at Hof, a handful of houses on the brow of a breezy hill, the church and tavern standing opposite to each other, and nothing between them but the dusty road, and the churchyard, with its iron crosses, and the fluttering tinsel of the funeral garlands. In the churchyard and at the tavern-door, were groups of peasants, waiting for divine service to begin. They were clothed in their holiday dresses. The men wore breeches and long boots, and frock-coats with large metal buttons; the women, straw hats, and gay calico gowns, with short waists and scant folds. They were adorned with a profusion of great, trumpery ornaments, and reminded Flemming of the Indians in the frontier villages of America. Near the churchyard-gate was a booth, filled with flaunting calicos; and opposite sat an old woman behind a table, which was loaded with ginger-bread. She had a roulette at her elbow, where the peasants risked a kreutzer for a cake. On other tables, cases of knives, scythes, reaping-hooks, and other implements of husbandry were offered for sale.

The travellers continued their journey, without stopping to hear mass. In the course of the forenoon they came suddenly in sight of the beautiful Lake of Saint Wolfgang, lying deep beneath them in the valley. On its shore, under them, sat the white village of Saint Gilgen, like a swan upon its reedy nest. They seemed to have taken it unawares, and as it were clapped their hands upon it in its sleep, and almost expected to see it spread its broad, snow-white wings, and fly away. The whole scene was one of surpassing beauty.

They drove leisurely down the steep hill, and stopped at the village inn. Before the door was a magnificent, broad-armed tree, with benches and tables beneath its shadow. On the front of the house was written in large letters, "Post-Tavern by Franz Schoendorfer"; and over this was a large sun-dial, and a half-effaced painting of a bear-hunt, covering the whole side of the house, and mostly red. Just as they drove up, a procession of priests with banners, and peasants with their hats in their hands, passed by towards the church. They were singing a solemn psalm. At the same moment, a smart servant girl, with a black straw hat, set coquettishly on her flaxen hair, and a large silver spoon stuck in her girdle, came out of the tavern, and asked Flemming what he would please to order for breakfast.

Breakfast was soon ready, and was served up at the head of the stairs, on an old-fashioned oaken table in the great hall, into which the chambers opened. Berkley ordered at the same time a tub of cold water, in which he seated himself, with his coat on, and a bed-quilt thrown round his knees. Thus he sat for an hour; ate his breakfast, and smoked a pipe, and laughed a good deal. He then went to bed and slept till dinner time. Meanwhile Flemming sat in his chamber and read. It was a large room in the front of the house, looking upon the village and the lake. The windows were latticed, with small panes, and the window-sills filled with fragrant flowers.

At length the heat of the noon was over. Day, like a weary pilgrim, had reached the western gate of Heaven, and Evening stooped down to unloose the latchets of his sandal-shoon. Flemming and Berkley sallied forth to ramble by the borders of the lake. Down the cool, green glades and alleys, beneath the illuminated leaves of the forest, over the rising grounds, in the glimmering fretwork of sunshine and leaf-shadow,—an exhilarating walk! The cool evening air by the lake was like a bath. They drank the freshness of the hour in thirsty draughts, and their breasts heaved rejoicing and revived, after the feverish, long confinement of the sultry summer day. And there, too, lay the lake, so beautiful and still! Did it not recall, think ye, the lake of Thun?

On their return homeward they passed near the village churchyard.

"Let us go in and see how the dead rest," said Flemming, as they passed beneath the belfry of the church; and they went in, and lingered among the tombs and the evening shadows.

How peaceful is the dwelling-place of those who inhabit the green hamlets, and populous cities of the dead! They need no antidote for care,—nor armour against fate. No morning sun shines in at the closed windows, and awakens them, nor shall until the last great day. At most a straggling sunbeam creeps in through the crumbling wall of an old neglected tomb,—a strange visiter, that stays not long. And there they all sleep, the holy ones, with their arms crossed upon their breasts, or lying motionless by their sides,—not carved in marble by the hand of man, but formed in dust, by the hand of God. God's peace be with them. No one comes to them now, to hold them by the hand, and with delicate fingers smooth their hair. They heed no more the blandishments of earthly friendship. They need us not, however much we may need them. And yet they silently await our coming.

Beautiful is that season of life, when we can say, in the language of Scripture, "Thou hast the dew of thy youth." But of these flowers Death gathers many. He places them upon his bosom, and his form becomes transformed into something less terrific than before. We learn to gaze and shudder not; for he carries in his arms the sweet blossoms of our earthly hopes. We shall see them all again, blooming in a happier land.

Yes, Death brings us again to our friends. They are waiting for us, and we shall not live long. They have gone before us, and are like the angels in heaven. They stand upon the borders of the grave to welcome us, with the countenance of affection, which they wore on earth; yet more lovely, more radiant, more spiritual! O, he spake well who said, that graves are the foot-prints of angels.

Death has taken thee, too, and thou hast the dew of thy youth. He has placed thee upon his bosom, and his stern countenance wears a smile. The far country, toward which we journey, seems nearer to us, and the way less dark; for thou hast gone before, passing so quietly to thy rest, that day itself dies not more calmly!

It was in an hour of blessed communion with the souls of the departed, that the sweet poet Henry Vaughan wrote those few lines, which have made death lovely, and his own name immortal!

"They are all gone into a world of light,
And I alone sit lingering here!
Their very memory is fair and bright,
And my sad thoughts doth clear.

"It glows and glitters in my cloudy breast,
Like stars upon some gloomy grove,
Or those faint beams in which the hill is dressed,
After the sun's remove.

"I see them walking in an air of glory,
Whose light doth trample on my days,
My days, which are at best but dull and hoary,
Mere glimmerings and decays.

"O holy hope, and high humility,
High as the heavens above!
These are your walks, and ye have showed them me,
To kindle my cold love.

"Dear, beauteous Death! the jewel of the just!
Shining nowhere but in the dark!
What mysteries do lie beyond thy dust,
Could man outlook that mark!

"He that hath found some fledged bird's nest, may know,
At first sight, if the bird be flown;
But what fair field or grove he sings in now,
That is to him unknown.

"And yet as angels, in some brighter dreams,
Call to the soul, when man doth sleep,
So some strange thoughts transcend our wonted themes,
And into glory peep!"

Such were Flemming's thoughts, as he stood among the tombs at evening in the churchyard of Saint Gilgen. A holy calm stole over him. The fever of his heart was allayed. He had a moment's rest from pain; and went back to his chamber in peace. Whence came this holy calm, this long-desired tranquillity? He knew not; yet the place seemed consecrated. He resolved to linger there, beside the lake, which was a Pool of Bethesda for him; and let Berkley go on alone to the baths of Ischel. He would wait for him there in the solitude of Saint Gilgen. Long after they had parted for the night, he sat in his chamber, and thought of what he had suffered, and enjoyed the silence within and without. Hour after hour, slipped by unheeded, as he sat lost in his reverie. At length, his candle sank in its socket, gave one flickering gleam, and expired with a sob. This aroused him.

He went to the window, and peered out into the dark night. It was very late. Twice already since midnight had the great pulpit-orator Time, like a preacher in the days of the Puritans, turned the hour-glass on his high pulpit, the church belfry, and still went on with his sermon, thundering downward to the congregation in the churchyard and in the village. But they heard him not. They were all asleep in their narrow pews, namely, in their beds and in their graves. Soon afterward the cock crew; and the cloudy heaven, like the apostle, who denied his Lord, wept bitterly.

CHAPTER VI

SAINT WOLFGANG

The morning is lovely beyond expression. The heat of the sun is great; but a gentle wind cools the air. Birds never sang more loud and clear. The flowers, too, on the window-sill, and on the table, rose, geranium, and the delicate crimson cactus, are all so beautiful, that we think the German poet right, when he calls the flowers "stars in the firmament of the earth." Out of doors all is quiet. Opposite the window stands the village schoolhouse. There are two parasite trees, with their outspread branches nailed against the white walls, like the wings of culprit kites. There the rods grow. Under them, on a bench at the door, sit school-girls; and barefoot urchins in breeches are spelling out their lessons. The clock strikes twelve, and one by one they disappear, and go into the hive, like bees at the sound of a brass pan. At the door of the next house sits a poor woman, knitting in the shade; and in front of her is an aqueduct pouring its cool, clear water into a rough wooden trough. A travelling carriage without horses, stands at the inn-door, and a postilion in red jacket is talking with a blacksmith, who wears blue woollen stockings and a leather apron. Beyond is a stable, and still further a cluster of houses and the village church. They are repairing the belfry and the bulbous steeple. A little farther, over the roofs of the houses, you can see Saint Wolfgang's Lake. Water so bright and beautiful hardly flows elsewhere. Green, and blue, and silver-white run into each other, with almost imperceptible change, like the streaks on the sides of a mackerel. And above are the pinnacles of the mountains; some bald, and rocky, and cone-shaped, and others bold, and broad, and dark with pines.

Such was the scene, which Paul Flemming beheld from his window a few mornings after Berkley's departure. The quiet of the place had soothed him. He had become more calm. His heart complained less loudly in the holy village silence, as we are wont to lower our voices when those around us speak in whispers. He began to feel at times an interest in the lowly things around him. The face of the landscape pleased him, but more than this the face of the poor woman who sat knitting in the shade. It was a pale, meek countenance, with more delicacy in its features than is usual among peasantry. It wore also an expression of patient suffering. As he was looking at her, a deformed child came out of the door and hung upon her knees. She caressed him affectionately. It was her child; in whom she beheld her own fair features distorted and hardly to be recognised, as one sometimes sees his face reflected from the bowl of a spoon.

The child's deformity and the mother's tenderness interested the feelings of Flemming. The landlady told him something of the poor woman's history. She was the widow of a blacksmith, who had died soon after their marriage. But she survived to become a mother, just as, in oaks, immediately after fecundation, the male flower fades and falls, while the female continues and ripens into perfect fruit. Alas! her child was deformed. Yet she looked upon him with eyes of maternal fondness and pity, loving him still more for his deformity. And in her heart she said, as the Mexicans say to their new-born

offspring, "Child, thou art come into the world to suffer. Endure, and hold thy peace." Though poor, she was not entirely destitute; for her husband had left her, beside the deformed child, a life estate in a tomb in the churchyard of Saint Gilgen. During the week she labored for other people, and on Sundays for herself, by going to church and reading the Bible. On one of the blank leaves she had recorded the day of her birth, and that of her child's, likewise her marriage and her husband's death. Thus she lived, poor, patient and resigned. Her heart was a passion-flower, bearing within it the crown of thorns and the cross of Christ. Her ideas of Heaven were few and simple. She rejected the doctrine that it was a place of constant activity, and not of repose, and believed, that, when she at length reached it, she should work no more, but sit always in a clean white apron, and sing psalms.

As Flemming sat meditating on these things, he paid new homage in his heart to the beauty and excellence of the female character. He thought of the absent and the dead; and said, with tears in his eyes;

"Shall I thank God for the green Summer, and the mild air, and the flowers, and the stars, and all that makes this world so beautiful, and not for the good and beautiful beings I have known in it? Has not their presence been sweeter to me than flowers? Are they not higher and holier than the stars? Are they not more to me than all things else?"

Thus the morning passed away in musings; and in the afternoon, when Flemming was preparing to go down to the lake, as his custom was, a carriage drew up before the door, and, to his great astonishment, out jumped Berkley. The first thing he did was to give the Postmaster, who stood near the door, a smart cut with his whip. The sufferer gently expostulated, saying,

"Pray, Sir, don't; I am lame."

Whereupon Berkley desisted, and began instead to shake the Postmaster's wife by the shoulders, and order his dinner in English. But all this was done so good-naturedly, and with such a rosy, laughing face, that no offence was taken.

"So you have returned much sooner than you intended;" said Flemming, after the first friendly salutations.

"Yes," replied Berkley; "I got tired of Ischel,—very tired. I did not find the friends there, whom I expected. Now I am going back to Salzburg, and then to Gastein. There I shall certainly find them. You must go with me."

Flemming declined the invitation; and proposed to Berkley, that he should join him in his excursion on the lake.

"You shall hear the grand echo of the Falkenstein," said he, "and behold the scene of the Bridal Tragedy; and then we will go on as far as the village of Saint Wolfgang, which you have not yet seen, except across the lake."

"Well, this afternoon I devote to you; for to-morrow we part once more, and who knows when we shall meet again?"

They went down to the water's side without farther delay; and, taking a boat with two oars, struck across an elbow of the lake towards a barren rock by the eastern shore, from which a small white monument shone in the sun.

"That monument," said one of the boatmen, a stout young lad in leather breeches, "was built by a butcher, to the glory of Saint Wolfgang, who saved him from drowning. He was one day riding an ox to market along the opposite bank; when the animal taking fright, sprang into the water, and swam over to this place, with the butcher on his back."

"And do you think he could have done this," asked Berkley; "if Saint Wolfgang had not helped him?"

"Of course not!" answered leather-breeches; and the Englishman laughed.

From this point they rowed along under the shore to a low promontory, upon which stood another monument, commemorating a more tragical event.

"This is the place I was speaking of," said Flemming, as the boatmen rested on their oars. "The melancholy and singular event it commemorates happened more than two centuries ago. There was a bridal party here upon the ice one winter; and in the midst of the dance the ice broke, and the whole merry company were drowned together, except the fiddlers, who were sitting on the shore."

They looked in silence at the monument, and at the blue quiet water, under which the bones of the dancers lay buried, hand in hand. The monument is of stone, painted white, with an over-hanging roof to shelter it from storms. In a niche in front is a small image of the Saviour, in a sitting posture; and an inscription, upon a marble tablet below, says that it was placed there by Longinus Walther and his wife Barbara Juliana von Hainberg; themselves long since peacefully crumbled to dust, side by side in some churchyard.

"That was breaking the ice with a vengeance!" said Berkley, as they pushed out into the lake again; and ere long they were floating beneath the mighty precipice of Falkenstein; a steep wall of rock, crowned with a chapel and a hermitage, where in days of old lived the holy Saint Wolfgang. It is now haunted only by an echo, so distinct and loud, that one might imagine the ghost of the departed saint to be sitting there, and repeating the voices from below, not word by word, but sentence by sentence, as if he were passing them up to the recording angel.

"Ho! ho! ho!" shouted Berkley; and the sound seemed to strike the wall of stone, like the flapping of steel plates; "Ho! ho! ho! How are you to-day, Saint Wolfgang! You infernal old rascal! How is the Frau von Wolfgang!—God save great George the King! Damn your eyes! Hold your tongue! Ho! ho! ha! ha! hi!"

And the words were recorded above; and a voice repeated them with awful distinctness in the blue depths overhead, and Flemming felt in his inmost soul the contrast between the holy heavens, and the mockery of laughter, and the idle words, which fall back from the sky above us and soil not its purity.

In half an hour they were at the village of Saint Wolfgang, threading a narrow street, above which the roofs of quaint, picturesque old houses almost met. It led them to a Gothic church; a magnificent one for a village;—in front of which was a small court, shut in by Italian-looking houses, with balconies, and flowers at the windows. Here a bronze fountain of elaborate workmanship was playing in the shade. On

its summit stood an image of the patron Saint of the village; and, running round the under lip of the water-basin below, they read this inscription in old German rhymes;

"I am in the honor of Saint Wolfgang raised. Abbot Wolfgang Habel of Emensee, he hath made me for the use and delight of poor pilgrim wight. Neither gold nor wine hath he; at this water shall he merry be. In the year of the Lord fifteen hundred and fifteen, hath the work completed been. God be praised!"

As they were deciphering the rude characters of this pious inscription, a village priest came down a high flight of steps from the parsonage near the church, and courteously saluted the strangers. After returning the salutation, the mad Englishman, without preface, asked him how many natural children were annually born in the parish. The question seemed to astonish the good father, but he answered it civilly, as he did several other questions, which Flemming thought rather indiscreet, to say the least.

"You will excuse our curiosity," said he to the priest, by way of apology. "We are strangers from distant countries. My friend is an Englishman and I an American."

Berkley, however, was not so easily silenced. After a few moments' conversation he broke out into most audacious Latin, in which the only words clearly intelligible were;

"Plurimum reverende, in Christo religiosissime, ac clarissime Domine, necnon et amice observandissime! Petrus sic est locutus; 'Nec argentum mihi, nec aurum est; sed quod habeo, hoc tibi do; surge et ambula.'"

He seemed to be speaking of the fountain. The priest answered meekly,

"Non intellexi, Domine!"

But Berkley continued with great volubility to speak of his being a stranger in the land, and all men being strangers upon earth, and hoping to meet the good priest hereafter in the kingdom of Heaven. The priest seemed confounded, and abashed. Through the mist of a strange pronunciation he could recognise only here and there a familiar word. He took out his snuff-box; and tried to quote a passage from Saint Paul;

"Ut dixit Sanctus Paulus; qui bene facit—"

Here his memory failed him, or, as the French say, he was at the end of his Latin, and, stretching forth his long forefinger, he concluded in German;

"Yes;—I don't—so clearly remember—what he did say."

The Englishman helped him through with a moral phrase; and then pulling off his hat, exclaimed very solemnly;

"Vale, domine doctissime et reverendissime!"

And the Dominie, as if pursued by a demon, made a sudden and precipitate retreat down a flight of steps into the street.

"There!" said Berkley laughing, "I beat him at his own weapons. What do you say of my Latin?"

"I say of it," replied Flemming, "what Holophernes said of Sir Nathaniel's; 'Priscian a little scratched; 't will serve.' I think I have heard better. But what a whim! I thought I should have laughed aloud."

They were still sitting by the bronze fountain when the priest returned, accompanied by a short man, with large feet, and a long blue surt out, so greasy, that it reminded one of Polilla's in the Spanish play, which was lined with slices of pork. His countenance was broad and placid, but his blue eyes gleamed with a wild, mysterious, sorrowful expression. Flemming thought the Latin contest was to be renewed, with more powder and heavier guns. He was mistaken. The stranger saluted him in German, and said, that, having heard he was from America, he had come to question him about that distant country, for which he was on the point of embarking. There was nothing peculiar in his manner, nor in the questions he asked, nor the remarks he made. They were the usual questions and remarks about cities and climate, and sailing the sea. At length Flemming asked him the object of his journey to America. The stranger came close up to him, and lowering his voice, said very solemnly;

"That holy man, Frederick Baraga, missionary among the Indians at Lacroix, on Lake Superior, has returned to his father-land, Krain; and I am chosen by Heaven to go forth as Minister Extraordinary of Christ, to unite all nations and people in one church!"

Flemming almost started at the singular earnestness, with which he uttered these words; and looked at him attentively, thinking to see the face of a madman. But the modest, unassuming look of that placid countenance was unchanged; only in the eyes burned a mysterious light, as if candles had been lighted in the brain, to magnify the daylight there.

"It is truly a high vocation," said he in reply. "But are you sure, that this is no hallucination? Are you certain, that you have been chosen by Heaven for this great work?"

"I am certain," replied the German, in a tone of great calmness and sincerity; "and, if Saint Peter and Saint Paul should come down from Heaven to assure me of it, my faith would be no stronger than it now is. It has been declared to me by many signs and wonders. I can no longer doubt, nor hesitate. I have already heard the voice of the Spirit, speaking to me at night; and I know that I am an apostle; and chosen for this work."

Such was the calm enthusiasm with which he spoke, that Flemming could not choose but listen. He felt interested in this strange being. There was something awe-inspiring in the spirit that possessed him. After a short pause he continued;

"If you wish to know who I am, I can tell you in few words. I think you will not find the story without interest."

He then went on to relate the circumstances recorded in the following chapter.

CHAPTER VII

THE STORY OF BROTHER BERNARDUS

"I was born in the city of Stein, in the land of Krain. My pious mother Gertrude sang me psalms and spiritual songs in childhood; and often, when I awoke in the night, I saw her still sitting, patiently at her work by the stove, and heard her singing those hymns of heaven, or praying in the midnight darkness when her work was done. It was for me she prayed. Thus, from my earliest childhood, I breathed the breath of pious aspirations. Afterwards I went to Laybach as a student of theology; and after the usual course of study, was ordained a priest. I went forth to the care of souls; my own soul filled with the faith, that ere long all people would be united in one church. Yet at times my heart was heavy, to behold how many nations there are who have not heard of Christ; and how those, who are called Christians, are divided into numberless sects, and how among these are many who are Christians in name only. I determined to devote myself to the great work of the one church universal; and for this purpose, to give myself wholly up to the study of the Evangelists and the Fathers. I retired to the Benedictine cloister of Saint Paul in the valley of Lavant. The father-confessor in the nunnery of Laak, where I then lived, strengthened me in this resolve. I had long walked with this angel of God in a human form, and his parting benediction sank deep into my soul. The Prince-Abbot Berthold, of blessed memory, was then head of the Benedictine convent. He received me kindly, and led me to the library; where I gazed with secret rapture on the vast folios of the Christian Fathers, from which, as from an arsenal, I was to draw the weapons of holy warfare. In the study of these, the year of my noviciate passed. I became a Franciscan friar; and took the name of Brother Bernardus. Yet my course of life remained unchanged. I seldom left the cloister; but sat in my cell, and pored over those tomes of holy wisdom. About this time the aged confessor in Laak departed this life. His death was made known to me in a dream. It must have been after midnight, when I thought that I came into the church, which was brilliantly lighted up. The dead body of the venerable saint was brought in, attended by a great crowd. It seemed to me, that I must go up into the pulpit and pronounce his funeral oration; and, as I ascended the stairs, the words of my text came into my mind; 'Blessed in the sight of the Lord is the death of his saints.' My funeral sermon ended in a strain of exultation; and I awoke with 'Amen!' upon my lips. A few days afterwards, I heard that on that night the old man died. After this event I became restless and melancholy. I strove in vain to drive from me my gloomy thoughts. I could no longer study. I was no longer contented in the cloister. I even thought of leaving it.

"One night I had gone to bed early, according to my custom, and had fallen asleep. Suddenly I was awakened by a bright and wonderful light, which shone all about me, and filled me with heavenly rapture. Shortly after I heard a voice, which pronounced distinctly these words, in the Sclavonian tongue; 'Remain in the cloister!' It was the voice of my departed mother. I was fully awake; yet saw nothing but the bright light, which disappeared, when the words had been spoken. Still it was broad daylight in my chamber. I thought I had slept beyond my usual hour. I looked at my watch. It was just one o'clock after midnight. Suddenly the daylight vanished, and it was dark. In the morning I arose, as if new-born, through the wonderful light, and the words of my mother's voice. It was no dream. I knew it was the will of God that I should stay; and I could again give myself up to quiet study. I read the whole Bible through once more in the original text; and went on with the Fathers, in chronological order. Often, after the apparition of the light, I awoke at the same hour; and though I heard no voice and saw no light, yet was refreshed with heavenly consolation.

"Not long after this an important event happened in the cloister. In the absence of the deacon of the Abbey, I was to preach the Thanksgiving sermon of Harvest-home. During the week the Prince-Abbot Berthold gave up the ghost; and my sermon became at once a Thanks-giving and Funeral Sermon. Perhaps it may not be unworthy of notice, that I was thus called to pronounce the burial discourse over

the body of the last reigning, spiritual Prince Abbot in Germany. He was a man of God, and worthy of this honor.

"One year after this event, I was appointed Professor of Biblical Hermeneutics in Klagenfurt, and left the Abbey forever. In Klagenfurt I remained ten years, dwelling in the same house, and eating at the same table, with seventeen other professors. Their conversation naturally suggested new topics of study, and brought to my notice books, which I had never before seen. One day I heard at table, that Maurus Cappellari, a monk of Camaldoli, had been elected Pope, under the name of Gregory Sixteenth. He was spoken of as a very learned man, who had written many books. At this time I was a firm believer in the Pope's infallibility; and when I heard these books mentioned, there arose in me an irresistible longing to read them. I inquired for them; but they were nowhere to be had. At length I heard, that his most important work, The Triumph of the Holy See, and of the Church, had been translated into German and published in Augsburg. Ere long the precious volume was in my hands. I began to read it with the profoundest awe. The farther I read, the more my wonder grew. The subject was of the deepest interest to me. I could not lay the book out of my hand, till I had read it through with the closest attention. Now at length my eyes were opened. I saw before me a monk, who had been educated in an Italian cloister; who, indeed, had read much, and yet only what was calculated to strengthen him in the prejudices of his childhood; and who had entirely neglected those studies upon which a bishop should most rely, in order to work out the salvation of man. I perceived at the same time, that this was the strongest instrument for battering down the walls, which separate Christian from Christian. I saw, though as yet dimly, the way in which the union of Christians in the one true church was to be accomplished. I knew not whether to be most astonished at my own blindness, that, in all my previous studies, I had not perceived, what the reading of this single book made manifest to me; or at the blindness of the Pope, who had undertaken to justify such follies, without perceiving that at the same moment he was himself lying in fatal error. But since I have learned more thoroughly the ways of the Lord, I am now no more astonished at this, but pray only to Divine providence, who so mysteriously prepares all people to be united in one true church. I no longer believed in the Pope's infallibility; nay, I believed even, that, to the great injury of humanity, he lay in fatal error. I felt, moreover, that now the time had fully come, when I should publicly show myself, and found in America a parish and a school, and become the spiritual guide of men, and the schoolmaster of children.

"It was then, and on that account, that I wrote in the Latin tongue my great work on Biblical Hermeneutics. But in Germany it cannot be published. The Austrian censor of the press cannot find time to read it, though I think, that if I have spent so many laborious days and sleepless nights in writing it, this man ought likewise to find time enough not only to read it, but to examine all the grounds of my reasoning, and point out to me any errors, if he can find any. Notwithstanding, the Spirit gave me no repose, but urged me ever mightily on to the perfection of my great work.

"One morning I sat writing, under peculiar influences of the Spirit, upon the Confusion of Tongues, the Division of the People, and the importance of the study of Comparative Philology, in reference to their union in one church. So wrapped was I in the thought, that I came late into my lecture-room; and after lecture returned to my chamber, where I wrote till the clock struck twelve. At dinner, one of the Professors asked if any one had seen the star, about which so much was said. The Professor of Physics, said, that the student Johannes Schminke had come to him in the greatest haste, and besought him to go out and see the wonderful star; but, being incredulous about it, he made no haste, and, when they came into the street, the star had disappeared. When I heard the star spoken of, my soul was filled with rapture; and a voice within me seemed to say, 'The great time is approaching; labor unweariedly in thy work.' I sought out the student; and like Herod, inquired diligently what time the star appeared. He

informed me, that, just as the clock was striking eight, in the morning, he went out of his house to go to the college, and saw on the square a crowd looking at a bright star. It was the very hour, when I was writing alone in my chamber on the importance of Comparative Philology in bringing about the union of all nations. I felt, that my hour had come. Strangely moved, I walked up and down my chamber. The evening twilight came on. I lighted my lamp, and drew the green curtains before the windows, and sat down to read. But hardly had I taken the book into my hand, when the Spirit began to move me, and urge me then to make my last decision and resolve. I made a secret vow, that I would undertake the voyage to America. Suddenly my troubled thoughts were still. An unwonted rapture filled my heart. I sat and read till the supper bell rang. They were speaking at table of a red glaring meteor, which had just been seen in the air, southeast from Klagenfurt; and had suddenly disappeared with a dull, hollow sound. It was the very moment at which I had taken my final resolution to leave my native land. Every great purpose and event of my life, seemed heralded and attended by divine messengers; the voices of the dead; the bright morning star, shining in the clear sunshine; and the red meteor in the evening twilight.

"I now began seriously to prepare for my departure. The chamber I occupied, had once been the library of a Franciscan convent. Only a thick wall separated it from the church. In this wall was a niche, with heavy folding-doors, which had served the Franciscans as a repository for prohibited books. Here also I kept my papers, and my great work on Biblical Hermeneutics. The inside of the doors was covered with horrible caricatures of Luther, Melancthon, Calvin, and other great men. I used often to look at them with the deepest melancholy, when I thought that these great men likewise had labored upon earth, and fought with Satan in the church. But they were persecuted, denounced, condemned to die. So perhaps will it be with me. I thought of this often; and armed myself against the fear of death. I was in constant apprehension, lest the police should search my chamber during my absence, and, by examining my papers, discover my doctrine and designs. But the Spirit said to me; 'Be of good cheer; I will so blind the eyes of thy enemies, that it shall not once occur to them to think of thy writings.'

"At length, after many difficulties and temptations of the Devil, I am on my way to America. Yesterday I took leave of my dearest friend, Gregory Kuscher, in Hallstadt. He seemed filled with the Spirit of God, and has wonderfully strengthened me in my purpose. All the hosts of heaven looked on, and were glad. The old man kissed me at parting; and I ascended the mountain as if angels bore me up in their arms. Near the summit, lay a newly fallen avalanche, over which, as yet, no footsteps had passed. This was my last temptation. 'Ha!' cried I aloud, 'Satan has prepared a snare for me; but I will conquer him with godly weapons.' I sprang over the treacherous snow, with greater faith than St. Peter walked the waters of the Lake of Galilee; and came down the valley, while the mountain peaks yet shone in the setting sun. God smiles upon me. I go forth, full of hopeful courage. On Christmas next, I shall excommunicate the Pope."

Saying these words, he slowly and solemnly took his leave, like one conscious of the great events which await him, and withdrew with the other priest into the church. Flemming could not smile as Berkley did; for in the solitary, singular enthusiast, who had just left them, he saw only another melancholy victim to solitude and over-labor of the brain; and felt how painful a thing it is, thus to become unconsciously the alms-man of other men's sympathies, a kind of blind beggar for the charity of a good wish or a prayer.

The sun was now setting. Silently they floated back to Saint Gilgen, amid the cool evening shadows. The village clock struck nine as they landed; and as Berkley was to depart early in the morning, he went to bed betimes. On bidding Flemming good night he said;

"I shall not see you in the morning; so good bye, and God bless you. Remember my parting words. Never mind trifles. In this world a man must either be anvil or hammer. Care killed a cat!"

"I have heard you say that so often," replied Flemming, laughing, "that I begin to believe it is true. But I wonder if Care shaved his left eyebrow, after doing the deed, as the ancient Egyptians used to do!"

"Aha! now you are sweeping cobwebs from the sky! Good night! Good night!"

A sorrowful event happened in the neighbourhood that night. The widow's child died suddenly. "Woe is me!"—thus mourns the childless mother in one of the funeral songs of Greenland; "Woe is me, that I should gaze upon thy place and find it vacant! In vain for thee thy mother dries the sea-drenched garments!" Not in these words, but in thoughts like these, did the poor mother bewail the death of her child, thinking mostly of the vacant place, and the daily cares and solicitudes of maternal love. Flemming saw a light in her chamber, and shadows moving to and fro, as he stood by the window, gazing into the starry, silent sky. But he little thought of the awful domestic tragedy, which was even then enacted behind those thin curtains!

CHAPTER VIII

FOOT-PRINTS OF ANGELS

It was Sunday morning; and the church bells were all ringing together. From all the neighbouring villages, came the solemn, joyful sounds, floating through the sunny air, mellow and faint and low,—all mingling into one harmonious chime, like the sound of some distant organ in heaven. Anon they ceased; and the woods, and the clouds, and the whole village, and the very air itself seemed to pray, so silent was it everywhere.

Two venerable old men,—high priests and patriarchs were they in the land,—went up the pulpit stairs, as Moses and Aaron went up Mount Hor, in the sight of all the congregation,—for the pulpit stairs were in front, and very high.

Paul Flemming will never forget the sermon he heard that day,—no, not even if he should live to be as old as he who preached it. The text was, "I know that my Redeemer liveth." It was meant to console the pious, poor widow, who sat right below him at the foot of the pulpit stairs, all in black, and her heart breaking. He said nothing of the terrors of death, nor of the gloom of the narrow house, but, looking beyond these things, as mere circumstances to which the imagination mainly gives importance, he told his hearers of the innocence of childhood upon earth, and the holiness of childhood in heaven, and how the beautiful Lord Jesus was once a little child, and now in heaven the spirits of little children walked with him, and gathered flowers in the fields of Paradise. Good old man! In behalf of humanity, I thank thee for these benignant words! And, still more than I, the bereaved mother thanked thee, and from that hour, though she wept in secret for her child, yet

"She knew he was with Jesus,
And she asked him not again."

After the sermon, Paul Flemming walked forth alone into the churchyard. There was no one there, save a little boy, who was fishing with a pin hook in a grave half full of water. But a few moments afterward, through the arched gateway under the belfry, came a funeral procession. At its head walked a priest in white surplice, chanting. Peasants, old and young, followed him, with burning tapers in their hands. A young girl carried in her arms a dead child, wrapped in its little winding sheet. The grave was close under the wall, by the church door. A vase of holy water stood beside it. The sexton took the child from the girl's arms, and put it into a coffin; and, as he placed it in the grave, the girl held over it a cross, wreathed with roses, and the priest and peasants sang a funeral hymn. When this was over, the priest sprinkled the grave and the crowd with holy water; and then they all went into the church, each one stopping as he passed the grave to throw a handful of earth into it, and sprinkle it with holy water.

A few moments afterwards, the voice of the priest was heard saying mass in the church, and Flemming saw the toothless old sexton treading the fresh earth into the grave of the little child, with his clouted shoes. He approached him, and asked the age of the deceased. The sexton leaned a moment on his spade, and shrugging his shoulders replied;

"Only an hour or two. It was born in the night, and died this morning early?"

"A brief existence," said Flemming. "The child seems to have been born only to be buried, and have its name recorded on a wooden tombstone."

The sexton went on with his work, and made no reply. Flemming still lingered among the graves, gazing with wonder at the strange devices, by which man has rendered death horrible and the grave loathsome.

In the Temple of Juno at Elis, Sleep and his twin-brother Death were represented as children reposing in the arms of Night. On various funeral monuments of the ancients the Genius of Death is sculptured as a beautiful youth, leaning on an inverted torch, in the attitude of repose, his wings folded and his feet crossed. In such peaceful and attractive forms, did the imagination of ancient poets and sculptors represent death. And these were men in whose souls the religion of Nature was like the light of stars, beautiful, but faint and cold! Strange, that in later days, this angel of God, which leads us with a gentle hand, into the "Land of the great departed, into the silent Land," should have been transformed into a monstrous and terrific thing! Such is the spectral rider on the white horse;—such the ghastly skeleton with scythe and hour-glass;—the Reaper, whose name is Death!

One of the most popular themes of poetry and painting in the Middle Ages, and continuing down even into modern times, was the Dance of Death. In almost all languages is it written,—the apparition of the grim spectre, putting a sudden stop to all business, and leading men away into the "remarkable retirement" of the grave. It is written in an ancient Spanish Poem, and painted on a wooden bridge in Switzerland. The designs of Holbein are well known. The most striking among them is that, where, from a group of children sitting round a cottage hearth, Death has taken one by the hand, and is leading it out of the door. Quietly and unresisting goes the little child, and in its countenance no grief, but wonder only; while the other children are weeping and stretching forth their hands in vain towards their departing brother. A beautiful design it is, in all save the skeleton. An angel had been better, with folded wings, and torch inverted!

And now the sun was growing high and warm. A little chapel, whose door stood open, seemed to invite Flemming to enter and enjoy the grateful coolness. He went in. There was no one there. The walls were

covered with paintings and sculpture of the rudest kind, and with a few funeral tablets. There was nothing there to move the heart to devotion; but in that hour the heart of Flemming was weak,—weak as a child's. He bowed his stubborn knees, and wept. And oh! how many disappointed hopes, how many bitter recollections, how much of wounded pride, and unrequited love, were in those tears, through which he read on a marble tablet in the chapel wall opposite, this singular inscription;

"Look not mournfully into the Past. It comes not back again. Wisely improve the Present. It is thine. Go forth to meet the shadowy Future, without fear, and with a manly heart."

It seemed to him, as if the unknown tenant of that grave had opened his lips of dust, and spoken to him the words of consolation, which his soul needed, and which no friend had yet spoken. In a moment the anguish of his thoughts was still. The stone was rolled away from the door of his heart; death was no longer there, but an angel clothed in white. He stood up, and his eyes were no more bleared with tears; and, looking into the bright, morning heaven, he said;

"I will be strong!"

Men sometimes go down into tombs, with painful longings to behold once more the faces of their departed friends; and as they gaze upon them, lying there so peacefully with the semblance, that they wore on earth, the sweet breath of heaven touches them, and the features crumble and fall together, and are but dust. So did his soul then descend for the last time into the great tomb of the Past, with painful longings to behold once more the dear faces of those he had loved; and the sweet breath of heaven touched them, and they would not stay, but crumbled away and perished as he gazed. They, too, were dust. And thus, far-sounding, he heard the great gate of the Past shut behind him as the Divine Poet did the gate of Paradise, when the angel pointed him the way up the Holy Mountain; and to him likewise was it forbidden to look back.

In the life of every man, there are sudden transitions of feeling, which seem almost miraculous. At once, as if some magician had touched the heavens and the earth, the dark clouds melt into the air, the wind falls, and serenity succeeds the storm. The causes which produce these sudden changes may have been long at work within us, but the changes themselves are instantaneous, and apparently without sufficient cause. It was so with Flemming; and from that hour forth he resolved, that he would no longer veer with every shifting wind of circumstance; no longer be a child's plaything in the hands of Fate, which we ourselves do make or mar. He resolved henceforward not to lean on others; but to walk self-confident and self-possessed; no longer to waste his years in vain regrets, nor wait the fulfilment of boundless hopes and indiscreet desires; but to live in the Present wisely, alike forgetful of the Past, and careless of what the mysterious Future might bring. And from that moment he was calm, and strong; he was reconciled with himself! His thoughts turned to his distant home beyond the sea. An indescribable, sweet feeling rose within him.

"Thither will I turn my wandering footsteps," said he; "and be a man among men, and no longer a dreamer among shadows. Henceforth be mine a life of action and reality! I will work in my own sphere, nor wish it other than it is. This alone is health and happiness. This alone is Life;

'Life that shall send
A challenge to its end,
And when it comes, say, Welcome, friend!'

Why have I not made these sage reflections, this wise resolve, sooner? Can such a simple result spring only from the long and intricate process of experience? Alas! it is not till Time, with reckless hand, has torn out half the leaves from the Book of Human Life, to light the fires of passion with, from day to day, that Man begins to see, that the leaves which remain are few in number, and to remember, faintly at first, and then more clearly, that, upon the earlier pages of that book, was written a story of happy innocence, which he would fain read over again. Then come listless irresolution, and the inevitable inaction of despair; or else the firm resolve to record upon the leaves that still remain, a more noble history, than the child's story, with which the book began."

CHAPTER IX

THE LAST PANG

"Farewell to thee, Saint Gilgen!" said Flemming, as he turned on the brow of the hill, to take his last look at the lake and the village below, and felt that this was one of the few spots on the wide earth to which he could say farewell with regret. "Thy majestic hills have impressed themselves upon my soul, as a seal upon wax. The quiet beauty of thy lake shall be to me forever an image of peace and purity and stillness, and that inscription in thy little churchyard, a sentence of wisdom for my after life."

Before the setting of the same sun, which then shone on that fair landscape, he was far on his way towards Munich. He had left far behind him the mountains of the Tyrol; and beheld them for the last time in the soft evening twilight, their bases green with forest trees, and here and there, a sharp rocky spire, and a rounded summit capped with snow. There they lay, their backs, like the backs of camels; a mighty caravan, reposing at evening in its march across the desert.

From Munich he passed through Augsburg and Ulm, on his way to Stuttgard. At the entrances of towns and villages, he saw large crucifixes; and on the fronts of many houses, coarse paintings and images of saints. In Gunzburg three priests in black were slowly passing down the street, and women fell on their knees to receive their blessing. There were many beggars, too, in the streets; and an old man who was making hay in a field by the road-side, when he saw the carriage approaching, threw down his rake, and came tumbling over the ditch, with his hat held out in both hands, uttering the most dismal wail. The next day, the bright yellow jackets of the postilions, and the two great tassels of their bugle-horns, dangling down their backs, like two cauliflowers, told him he was in Würtemberg; and, late in the evening, he stopped at a hotel in Stuttgard; and from his chamber-window, saw, in the bright moonlight, the old Gothic cathedral, with its narrow, lancet windows and jutting buttresses, right in front of him. Ere long he had forgotten all his cares and sorrows in sleep, and with them his hopes, and wishes, and good resolves.

He was still sitting at breakfast in his chamber, the next morning, when the great bell of the cathedral opposite began to ring, and reminded him that it was Sunday. Ere long the organ answered from within, and from its golden lips breathed forth a psalm. The congregation began to assemble, and Flemming went up with them to the house of the Lord. In the body of the church he found the pews all filled or locked; they seemed to belong to families. He went up into the gallery, and looked over the psalm-book of a peasant, while the congregation sang the sublime old hymn of Martin Luther,

"Our God, he is a tower of strength,

A trusty shield and weapon."

During the singing, a fat clergyman, clad in black, with a white surplice thrown loosely about him, came pacing along one of the aisles, from beneath the organ-loft and ascended the pulpit. After the hymn, he read a portion of Scripture, and then said;

"Let us unite in silent prayer."

And turning round, he knelt in the pulpit, while the congregation remained standing. For a while there was a breathless silence in the church, which to Flemming was more solemnly impressive than any audible prayer. The clergyman then arose, and began his sermon. His theme was the Reformation; and he attempted to prove how much easier it was to enter the kingdom of Heaven through the gateways of the Reformed Evangelical Dutch church, than by the aisles and penitential stair-cases of Saint Peter's. He then gave a history of the Reformation; and, when Flemming thought he was near the end, he heard him say, that he should divide his discourse into four heads. This reminded him of the sturdy old Puritan, Cotton Mather, who after preaching an hour, would coolly turn the hour-glass on the pulpit, and say; "Now, my beloved hearers, let us take another glass." He stole out into the silent, deserted street, and went to visit the veteran sculptor Dannecker. He found him in his parlour, sitting alone, with his psalm-book, and the reminiscences of a life of eighty years. As Flemming entered, he arose from the sofa, and tottered towards him; a venerable old man, of low stature, and dressed in a loose white jacket, with a face like Franklin's, his white hair flowing over his shoulders, and a pale, blue eye.

"So you are from America," said he. "But you have a German name. Paul Flemming was one of our old poets. I have never been in America, and never shall go there. I am now too old. I have been in Paris and in Rome. But that was long ago. I am now eight and seventy years old."

Here he took Flemming by the hand, and made him sit down by his side, on the sofa. And Flemming felt a mysterious awe creep over him, on touching the hand of the good old man, who sat so serenely amid the gathering shade of years, and listened to life's curfew-bell, telling, with eight and seventy solemn strokes, that the hour had come, when the fires of all earthly passion must be quenched within, and man must prepare to lie down and rest till the morning.

"You see," he continued, in a melancholy tone, "my hands are cold; colder than yours. They were warmer once. I am now an old man."

"Yet these are the hands," answered Flemming, "that sculptured the beauteous Ariadne and the Panther. The soul never grows old."

"Nor does Nature," said the old man, pleased with this allusion to his great work, and pointing to the green trees before his window. "This pleasure I have left to me. My sight is still good. I can even distinguish objects on the side of yonder mountain. My hearing is also unimpaired. For all which, I thank God."

Then, directing Flemming's attention to a fine engraving, which hung on the opposite wall of the room, he continued;

"That is an engraving of Canova's Religion. I love to sit here and look at it, for hours together. It is beautiful. He made the statue for his native town, where they had no church, until he built them one. He

placed the statue in it. This engraving he sent me as a present. Ah, he was a dear, good man. The name of his native town I have forgotten. My memory fails me. I cannot remember names."

Fearful that he had disturbed the old man in his morning devotions, Flemming did not remain long, but took his leave with regret. There was something impressive in the scene he had witnessed;—this beautiful old age of the artist; sitting by the open window, in the bright summer morning,—the labor of life accomplished, the horizon reached, where heaven and earth meet,—thinking it was angel's music, when he heard the church-bells ring; himself too old to go. As he walked back to his chamber, he thought within himself, whether he likewise might not accomplish something, which should live after him;—might not bring something permanent out of this fast-fleeting life of man, and then sit down, like the artist, in serene old age, and fold his hands in silence. He wondered how a man felt when he grew so old, that he could no longer go to church, but must sit at home and read the bible in large print. His heart was full of indefinite longings, mingled with regrets; longings to accomplish something worthy of life; regret, that as yet he had accomplished nothing, but had felt and dreamed only. Thus the warm days in spring bring forth passion-flowers and forget-me-nots. It is only after mid-summer, when the days grow shorter and hotter, that fruit begins to appear. Then, the heat of the day brings forward the harvest, and after the harvest, the leaves fall, and there is a gray frost. Much meditating upon these things, Paul Flemming reached his hotel. At that moment a person clad in green came down the church-steps, and crossed the street. It was the German student, of Interlachen. Flemming started as if a green snake had suddenly crossed his path. He took refuge in his chamber.

That night as he was sitting alone in his chamber, having made his preparation to depart the following morning, his attention was arrested by the sound of a female voice in the next room. A thin partition, with a door, separated it from his own. He had not before observed that the room was occupied. But, in the stillness of the night, the tones of that voice struck his ear. He listened. It was a lady, reading the prayers of the English Church. The tones were familiar; and awakened at once a thousand painfully sweet recollections. It was the voice of Mary Ashburton! His heart could not be deceived; and all its wounds began to bleed afresh, like those of a murdered man, when the murderer approaches. His first impulse was of affection only, boundless, irrepressible, delirious, as of old in the green valley of Interlachen. He waited for the voice to cease; that he might go to her, and behold her face once more. And then his pride rose up within him, and rebuked this weakness. He remembered his firm resolve; and blushed to find himself so feeble. And the voice ceased; and yet he did not go. Pride had so far gained the mastery over affection. He lay down upon his bed, like a child as he was. All about him was silence, and the silence was holy, for she was near; so near that he could almost hear the beating of her heart. He knew now for the first time how weak he was, and how strong his passion for that woman. His heart was like the altar of the Israelites of old; and, though drenched with tears, as with rain, it was kindled at once by the holy fire from heaven!

Towards morning he fell asleep, exhausted with the strong excitement; and, in that hour when, sleep being "nigh unto the soul," visions are deemed prophetic, he dreamed. O blessed vision of the morning, stay! thou wert so fair! He stood again on the green sunny meadow, beneath the ruined towers; and she was by his side, with her pale, speaking countenance and holy eyes; and he kissed her fair forehead; and she turned her face towards him beaming with affection and said, "I confess it now; you are the Magician!" and pressed him in a meek embrace, that he, "might rather feel than see the swelling of her heart." And then she faded away from his arms, and her face became transfigured, and her voice like the voice of an angel in heaven;—and he awoke, and was alone!

It was broad daylight; and he heard the postilion, and the stamping of horses' hoofs on the pavement at the door. At the same moment his servant came in, with coffee, and told him all was ready. He did not dare to stay. But, throwing himself into the carriage, he cast one look towards the window of the Dark Ladie, and a moment afterwards had left her forever! He had drunk the last drop of the bitter cup, and now laid the golden goblet gently down, knowing that he should behold it no more!

No more! O how majestically mournful are those words! They sound like the roar of the wind through a forest of pines!

Henry Wadsworth Longfellow was born on February 27th, 1807 in Portland, Maine (then part of Massachusetts) to Stephen Longfellow and Zilpah (nee Wadsworth) Longfellow. His father was a lawyer, and his maternal grandfather, Peleg Wadsworth, was a general in the American Revolutionary War and a Member of Congress.

It was a large family. Longfellow was the second of eight children; his siblings were Stephen (1805), Elizabeth (1808), Anne (1810), Alexander (1814), Mary (1816), Ellen (1818) and Samuel (1819).

Longfellow attended a dame school at the age of three and by age six was enrolled at the private Portland Academy. He was very studious and quickly became fluent in Latin. His mother encouraged his love of reading and learning and introduced him to many literary classics.

He published his first poem, a patriotic four-stanza affair entitled "The Battle of Lovell's Pond", in the Portland Gazette on November 17, 1820. He remained at the Portland Academy until he was fourteen. As a child, he spent much of his summers at his grandfather Peleg's farm in the nearby town of Hiram.

In the fall of 1822, the 15-year-old Longfellow enrolled at Bowdoin College in Brunswick, Maine. His grandfather was a founder of the college and his father a trustee. Here he met and befriended Nathaniel Hawthorne. Longfellow was already thinking of a career in literature. In his senior year he wrote to his father: "I will not disguise it in the least... the fact is, I most eagerly aspire after future eminence in literature, my whole soul burns most ardently after it, and every earthly thought centers in it... I am almost confident in believing, that if I can ever rise in the world it must be by the exercise of my talents in the wide field of literature."

Poetry was the writing form he felt most at ease with and he offered poems to many newspapers and magazines. Between January 1824 and graduation in 1825, he had almost 40 poems published, over half of which were in the short-lived Boston periodical The United States Literary Gazette.

When Longfellow graduated, he was ranked a pleasing fourth in the class, and had been elected to Phi Beta Kappa. He was quickly offered the post of professor of modern languages at his alma mater.

Accounts suggest that part of the requirement of acceptance was to tour Europe to become more immersed in both languages and cultures. Longfellow began his tour of Europe in May 1826 aboard the ship Cadmus. His travels in Europe would last three years and cost his father the princely sum of

$2,604.24. He visited France, Spain, Italy, Germany and England before returning to the United States in mid-August 1829.

His stock of languages now included French, Spanish, Portuguese, and German, and impressively, mostly without any formal instruction.

On August 27th, 1829, he wrote to the president of Bowdoin that he was turning down the professorship because he considered the $600 salary "disproportionate to the duties required". The trustees countered by raising the salary to $800 and an additional $100 to serve as the college's librarian, a post which required only one hour's attention a day.

On September 14th, 1831, Longfellow married Mary Storer Potter, a childhood friend from Portland. The couple settled in Brunswick. Longfellow now published several non-fiction and fiction prose pieces inspired by his friend Washington Irving, whom he had met in Madrid during his travels, these included "The Indian Summer" and "The Bald Eagle" in 1833.

During his years teaching at the college, he translated textbooks in French, Italian and Spanish; his first published book was in 1833, a translation of the poetry of the medieval Spanish poet Jorge Manrique. A travel book, Outre-Mer: A Pilgrimage Beyond the Sea, was first published in serial form before a book edition in 1835.

In December 1834, Longfellow received a letter from Josiah Quincy III, president of Harvard College, offering him the Smith Professorship of Modern Languages with the condition that he first spend a year or so abroad. The Longfellow's set off for Europe. He would now be able to add German, Dutch, Danish, Swedish, Finnish, and Icelandic to his repertoire of languages.

During the trip they discovered that Mary was pregnant. Sadly, in October 1835, she miscarried some six months into the pregnancy. Then followed several weeks of illness and at the age of 22 on November 29th, 1835 she died. Longfellow had her body embalmed, placed in a lead coffin itself inside an oak coffin which was then shipped to Mount Auburn Cemetery near Boston. He wrote movingly "One thought occupies me night and day... She is dead—She is dead! All day I am weary and sad".

Back in the United States, Longfellow took up the professorship at Harvard. He was required to live in Cambridge, close to the campus and rented rooms at the Craigie House in the spring of 1837. The home, built in 1759, had once been the headquarters of George Washington during the Siege of Boston.

Longfellow now felt able to publish again, starting with the collection Voices of the Night in 1839. It was mainly comprised of translations together with nine original poems and seven poems written back in his teenage years.

His romantic interests also began to surface again. He had begun to court Frances 'Fanny' Appleton, daughter of the Boston industrialist Nathan Appleton. At first, the independent-minded Appleton was not interested in marriage but Longfellow was determined. In July 1839, he wrote to a friend: "Victory hangs doubtful. The lady says she will not! I say she shall! It is not pride, but the madness of passion".

In late 1839, Longfellow published Hyperion, a book in prose inspired by his trips abroad and his still unsuccessful courtship of Fanny Appleton. Amidst this, Longfellow fell into "periods of neurotic depression

with moments of panic" and required a six-month leave of absence from Harvard to attend a health spa in the former Marienberg Benedictine Convent at Boppard in Germany.

Ballads and Other Poems was published in 1841 and included "The Village Blacksmith" and "The Wreck of the Hesperus". His reputation as a poet, and a commercial one at that, was set.

Longfellow published a play in 1842, The Spanish Student, based on his memories from his time in Spain in the 1820s. A small collection, Poems on Slavery, was also published in 1842. This was Longfellow's first public support of abolitionism. However, as Longfellow himself said, the poems were "so mild that even a Slaveholder might read them without losing his appetite for breakfast". The New England Anti-Slavery Association, however, was satisfied enough with the intent of the collection to reprint it for their own distribution.

On May 10th, 1843, after seven years in pursuit, Longfellow received a letter from Fanny Appleton agreeing to marry him. He was elated and immediately walked 90 minutes to meet her at her house.

Nathan Appleton bought the Craigie House as a wedding present to the pair. Longfellow lived there for the rest of his life. His love for Fanny is evident from Longfellow's only love poem, the sonnet "The Evening Star", written in October 1845:

"O my beloved, my sweet Hesperus!
My morning and my evening star of love!"

He once attended a ball without her and said, "The lights seemed dimmer, the music sadder, the flowers fewer, and the women less fair."

Longfellow and Fanny had six children: Charles Appleton (1844), Ernest Wadsworth (1845), Fanny (1847, who died in infancy), Alice Mary (1850), Edith (1853), and Anne Allegra (1855).

Aware of his growing stature and his ability to influence others he also encouraged and supported many other translators. In 1845, he published The Poets and Poetry of Europe, a large 800-page compendium of translated works by other writers. Longfellow intended the anthology "to bring together, into a compact and convenient form, as large an amount as possible of those English translations which are scattered through many volumes, and are not accessible to the general reader".

On November 1st, 1847, the epic poem Evangeline was published.

Longfellow's literary income was now becoming quite substantial: in 1840, he had made $219 but by 1850 it had grown to a very promising $1,900.

On June 14th, 1853, Longfellow held a farewell dinner party at his Cambridge home for his great friend Nathaniel Hawthorne, who was preparing to move overseas.

In 1854, Longfellow retired from Harvard, devoting himself entirely to writing. He would be awarded an honorary doctorate of laws from Harvard in 1859.

The Song of Haiwatha, his epic poem, and perhaps his best known and enjoyed work was published in 1855.

On a hot July 9th day, 1861, Fanny was putting several locks of her children's hair into an envelope and making attempts to seal it with hot sealing wax while Longfellow took a nap. The circumstances of what happened next vary but the actuality is that Fanny's dress caught fire. Her screams awakened Longfellow who rushed to help her and threw a rug over her and stifled the flames with his own body as best he could, but Fanny was already horrifically burned.

A doctor was called and Fanny was taken to her room to recover. She was in and out of consciousness throughout the night and was also administered ether. The next morning, July 10th, 1861, she died shortly after 10 o'clock after asking for a cup of coffee.

Longfellow, in his effort to save her had also been badly burned and was unable to attend her funeral. His facial injuries required he stopped shaving. The ensuing beard now became the quintessential look that everyone remembers from pictures.

Devastated, he never fully recovered and sometimes resorted to laudanum and ether to ease the pain. He worried he would go insane and begged "not to be sent to an asylum" and noted that he was "inwardly bleeding to death". In the sonnet "The Cross of Snow" (1879), which he wrote eighteen years later he wrote:

"Such is the cross I wear upon my breast
These eighteen years, through all the changing scenes
And seasons, changeless since the day she died".

Longfellow spent several years translating Dante Alighieri's epic poem, The Divine Comedy. To aid him in perfecting the translation and reviewing proofs, he invited several friends to weekly meetings every Wednesday from 1864. This became known as the "Dante Club", and regulars included William Dean Howells, James Russell Lowell, Charles Eliot Norton and other occasional guests. The full three-volume translation was published in the spring of 1867, though Longfellow would continue to revise it. It was wildly popular and was re-printed four times in its first year.

By 1868, Longfellow's annual income was over a staggering $48,000.

Longfellow was also part of a group of Poets who became known as The Fireside Poets. The group included Longfellow, William Cullen Bryant, John Greenleaf Whittier, James Russell Lowell, and Oliver Wendell Holmes Snr. Occasionally Ralph Waldo Emerson is also placed among their number. The name "Fireside Poets" derives from poetry reading as a collective family entertainment of the times.

During the 1860s, Longfellow, still a committed abolitionist, also hoped for a coming together, a reconciliation, between the north and south after the dark days of the Civil War. When his son was wounded during the war, he wrote the poem "Christmas Bells", later the basis of the carol I Heard the Bells on Christmas Day.

In 1874, Samuel Cutler Ward helped him sell the poem "The Hanging of the Crane" to the New York Ledger for $3,000; it was the highest price ever paid for a poem. An astonishing sum. But Longfellow was worth it. His fame and audience were widespread and devoted.

Continuing in his hopes for a better and more united America he wrote in his journal in 1878: "I have only one desire; and that is for harmony, and a frank and honest understanding between North and South". Longfellow, despite his aversion to public speaking, took up an offer from Joshua Chamberlain to speak at his fiftieth reunion at Bowdoin College. Here he read the poem "Morituri Salutamus" so quietly that few could hear.

On August 22th, 1879, a female admirer who seemed to know little about his history, traveled to Longfellow's house in Cambridge and, unaware to whom she was speaking, asked Longfellow: "Is this the house where Longfellow was born?" Longfellow told her it was not. The visitor then asked if he had died here. "Not yet", he replied.

Much of Longfellow's work is recognized for its melody-like musicality. As he says, "what a writer asks of his reader is not so much to like as to listen".

Longfellow, like many others of the period, called for the development of high quality American literature. In his work, Kavanagh, a character says: "We want a national literature commensurate with our mountains and rivers... We want a national epic that shall correspond to the size of the country... We want a national drama in which scope shall be given to our gigantic ideas and to the unparalleled activity of our people... In a word, we want a national literature altogether shaggy and unshorn, that shall shake the earth, like a herd of buffaloes thundering over the prairies."

As a translator Longfellow was very impressive. His translation of Dante's The Divine Comedy became a requirement for those who wanted to be a part of high culture.

In 1874, Longfellow oversaw a 31-volume anthology called Poems of Places, collecting poems of several geographical locations; Europe, Asia, and the Arabian countries. It was a work of great educational endeavor but Emerson was disappointed and is said to have told Longfellow: "The world is expecting better things of you than this... You are wasting time that should be bestowed upon original production".

At this point in his life Longfellow could look back and see that his early collections, Voices of the Night and Ballads and Other Poems, had made him instantly popular. The New-Yorker called him "one of the very few in our time who has successfully aimed in putting poetry to its best and sweetest uses". The Southern Literary Messenger immediately put Longfellow "among the first of our American poets".

The rapidity with which American readers embraced Longfellow was unparalleled in publishing history in the United States. His popularity spread throughout Europe, his poems translated into Italian, French, German, and other languages.

Longfellow was the most popular poet of his day. As a friend once wrote to him, "no other poet was so fully recognized in his lifetime". Some of his works including "Paul Revere's Ride" and "The Song of Haiwatha" may have rewritten the facts but became essential parts of the American psyche and culture. He was so admired that on his 70th birthday in 1877 the atmosphere was that of a national holiday, with parades, speeches, and, of course, the reading of his poems.

Over the years, Longfellow's reputation came to include his personality; he was a gentle, placid, poetic soul. James Russell Lowell said, Longfellow had an "absolute sweetness, simplicity, and modesty". The reality was that Longfellow's life was much more difficult than was assumed. He suffered from neuralgia,

which caused him constant pain, and poor eyesight. The difficulties of coping with the loss of two wives also took its toll. He was very quiet, reserved, and private; in later years, he became increasingly unsocial and avoided leaving home if he could.

In March 1882, Longfellow went to bed with severe stomach pain. He endured the pain for several days with the help of opium.

Henry Wadsworth Longfellow died, surrounded by family, on Friday, March 24th, 1882. He had been suffering from peritonitis.

He is buried with both of his wives at Mount Auburn Cemetery in Cambridge, Massachusetts. At Longfellow's funeral, his friend Ralph Waldo Emerson called him "a sweet and beautiful soul".

At the time of his death, his estate was valued at $356,320.

In 1884, Longfellow became the first non-British writer for whom a sculpted bust was placed in Poet's Corner of Westminster Abbey in London; he remains the sole American poet thus represented.

Henry Wadsworth Longfellow – A Concise Bibliography

Outre-Mer: A Pilgrimage Beyond the Sea (Travelogue) (1835)
Hyperion, a Romance (1839)
The Spanish Student. A Play in Three Acts (1843)
Evangeline: A Tale of Acadie (poem) (1847)
Kavanagh (1849)
The Golden Legend (poem) (1851)
The Song of Hiawatha (poem) (1855)
The New England Tragedies (1868)
The Divine Tragedy (1871)
Christus: A Mystery (1872)
Aftermath (poem) (1873)
The Arrow and the Song (poem)

Poetry Collections

Voices of the Night (1839)
Ballads & Other Poems (1841)
Poems on Slavery (1842)
The Belfry of Bruges & Other Poems (1845)
The Seaside and the Fireside (1850)
The Poetical Works of Henry Wadsworth Longfellow (1852)
The Courtship of Miles Standish & Other Poems (1858)
Tales of a Wayside Inn (1863)
Birds of Passage (1863)
Household Poems (1865)

Flower-de-Luce (1867)
Three Books of Song (1872)
The Masque of Pandora & Other Poems (1875)
Kéramos & Other Poems (1878)
Ultima Thule (1880)
In the Harbor (1882)
Michel Angelo: A Fragment (incomplete; published posthumously)

Translations

Coplas de Don Jorge Manrique (Translation from Spanish) (1833)
Dante's Divine Comedy (Translation) (1867)

Anthologies

Poets and Poetry of Europe (Translations) (1845)
The Waif (1845)
Poems of Places (1874)